Vern Thiessen

Two
Plays

Apple

Blowfish

Vern Thiessen

Two Plays

Apple · Blowfish

Vern Thiessen

Playwrights Canada Press
Toronto • Canada

Playwrights Canada Press
The Canadian Drama Publisher
215 Spadina Avenue, Suite 230, Toronto, Ontario CANADA M5T 2C7
416-703-0013   fax 416-408-3402
orders@playwrightscanada.com • www.playwrightscanada.com

This book would be twice its cover price were it not for the support of Canadian taxpayers through the Government of Canada Book Publishing Industry Development Program, Canada Council for the Arts, Ontario Arts Council and the Ontario Media Development Corporation.

Front cover photos: *Apple* photo of Coralie Cairns by Russ Hewitt, *Blowfish* photo of John Kirkpatrick and Christine Hanson, used with permission of Northern Light Theatre, by Ellis Brothers Photography.
Cover design: JLArt
Production Editor: Michael Petrasek

Library and Archives Canada Cataloguing in Publication

Thiessen, Vern
    Vern Thiessen : two plays / by Vern Thiessen.

Includes Apple, originally published 2002 and Blowfish, originally published 1998.
ISBN 979-0-88754-768-3

I. Thiessen, Vern. Apple. II. Thiessen, Vern. Blowfish. III. Title.

PS8589.H4524T44 2007   C812'.54   C2007-905875-2

This book
was printed
on 100%
recycled stock.

First edition: December 2007.
Apple and *Blowfish* were first published by Playwrights Canada Press.
Printed and bound by AGMV Marquis at Quebec, Canada.

Lydia!

Thank you for
the friendship
the comradarie
the companionship
and for the hope
that a better, kinder,
sweeter world
exists when the next
morning comes!

Love,
Vera

Table of Contents

Apple

to Eden, for healing me

and

for Sandra, who I never met

Acknowledgements

I would like to thank the following organizations which have assisted in the development of this play: the Edmonton Community Lottery Board, the Alberta Foundation for the Arts, the Banff/ATP PlayRites Colony (1999), Workshop West's Springboards New Play Festival (2000), the New Play Festival at Playwrights Theatre Centre (2001) in Vancouver, the Alberta Playwriting Competition, Original Sin Productions, the Unconscious Collective, Alberta Playwrights Network, the board, staff and volunteers of Workshop West Theatre, and The Blue Heron Theatre in New York City.

I would also like to thank the following individuals for their assistance and commitment: Eden Philp, Trevor Schmidt, David Mann, Rachel Ditor, Chapelle Jaffe, Shona Neil, Doug Barron, Ardelle Striker, Leslie (Hoban) Blake, Greg Nelson, Aaron Bushkowsky, Katrina Dunn, Kathryn Bracht, Cavin Cunnigham, Trenna Keating, Bill Hales, Pheobe Jonas, Margaret Reed, Hamilton Clancy, Charles Northcote, Randy White, Michael Nathanson, Andy Houston, and all the actors, stage managers and designers involved with workshopping the play. A special thanks to Ron Jenkins, whose uncompromising passion and vision is truly inspiring.

Apple was commissioned by Workshop West Theatre, Edmonton in 1999. It was first produced by Workshop West on April 11, 2002 at the Kaasa Theatre, Edmonton with the following company:

ANDY   Shaun Johnston
EVELYN   Coralie Cairns
SAMANTHA   Daniela Vlaskalic

Directed by Ron Jenkins
Stage Managed by Cheryl Millikin
Set, Props, Costumes and Lighting Design by Narda McCarroll
Original Music and Sound Design by Dave Clarke
Production Manager: Scott Peters
Production Assistant: Tandi McLeod
Carpenters: Bobby Smale and Scott Peters
General Manager: Shona Neil

A shorter version of *Apple* was first produced by The Unconscious Collective at the 1998 Edmonton Fringe Festival.

• • •

The American premiere of *Apple* was produced by Profiles Theatre Company, Chicago in April 2007, with the following company:

ANDY   Darrell W. Cox
EVELYN   Amy Matheny
SAMANTHA   Brady Fuqua

Directed by Joe Jahraus
Assistant Director: Eric Burgher
Stage Managed by Mark Christopher
Set Design by Thad Hallstein
Lighting Design by Ron Seeley
Costume Design by Patrick Serrano
Live music by William Jason Raynovich

Characters

ANDY   a man
EVELYN   his wife
SAMANTHA a medical student

Production Notes

The play should flow from scene to scene, but not quickly. Scene breaks are only indicated for rehearsal purposes. Much of the play's action lies in the "unspoken." Although not all pauses are created equally, the term *pause* is an important aspect of the play's action and rhythm. Theatricality and non-naturalism in design is encouraged. Both Act One and Act Two should run *no less* than 40 minutes each. In the original production, the intermission and the first scene of Act Two were removed, in favour of the following movement/music sequence:

> *LYN stares across the lake. She begins to pare down,*
> *SAM and ANDY assisting her: skirt and blouse*
> *removed, replaced by a hospital gown; hair put up,*
> *replaced by a handkerchief; make-up wiped away,*
> *replaced with nothing but her skin.*

Potential producers are free to use either choice. Please consult the playwright's agent for any updates to the text before production.

ACT ONE

*ANDY overlooking the lake. SAM watches him. LYN
in a different world.*

ANDY   *(to audience)* I bite into her breast.

LYN   *(smiles)* Careful...

ANDY   She says. I bite into her breast. Testing her flesh. Teasing
her skin, tasting her fruit. Until her mind shudders....

LYN   Careful...

ANDY   *(smiles)* She says.

LYN   They're not apples.

• • •

SAM   Good morning. *(unsure)* As you can see, this seminar
will examine "Dysfunction in Cell Differentiation and
Proliferation." We tend to treat this as a... simple concept. But in fact, it is represented by a highly complex
sequence of events....

• • •

LYN   Hi.

ANDY   Hey.

LYN   *(surprised)* You're home.

ANDY   Yeah.

LYN   Christ what a day.

ANDY   Oh?

LYN   Goddamn bitch.

ANDY   Who.

LYN   Darlene.

ANDY   Ah.

LYN   Get groceries?

ANDY   No.

LYN   Shit. Trying to tell me how to do my job. There is nothing to eat in this house.

ANDY   Lyn, I...

LYN   Did you pick up the stuff?

ANDY   The...?

LYN   The dry cleaning?

ANDY   Oh. No.

LYN   Andy! I have a meeting first thing, I need that dry cleaning, I need it. I'm hungry, there's no food in the house, I've got a headache, did you pick up the Adv—?

ANDY   No.

LYN   Christ, I'm going to kill you. It's bad enough I have to deal with that bitch without—

ANDY   Sorry, but—

LYN   I said, "go fuck yourself," is what I said "Darlene." I mean I didn't say that but I did.

She relishes it.

"I don't give a shit," I said, "who your clients are, I have 'til tomorrow nine p.m. to close the deal, and that's how long we're going to take. I don't care, princess," I said, "who they are, or what they wear, or what constituency they represent, or what they look like, or who they play golf with or who they fuck. I don't care." I have a responsibility to my client, the ball's in my court, I'm going to play it. "So don't try to rush me or push me or pull any of that political bullshit—" *(to ANDY)* You didn't wear that today did you?

She presses on.

So what happens? She goes off on some thing, some tangent, telling me I don't know what I'm doing. Me.

I don't know what I'm doing! "These people," she says, "they're this, they're that, they're blah blah blah, you can't do this to people like this." Well guess what. I've

been in this business fifteen years and fuck if I'm
going to be pushed around by some airhead thinks she
knows something. She knows shit, and she knows she
knows shit, and so I say, "Darlene: you know shit.
That's why I'm number one in the city, and you, honey,
are a fucking bottom-dweller. You want some advice?"
I say, "Do some sit-ups, for Christ sakes, get a fucking
makeover." And know what she does then? Know what
she does?

ANDY   Lyn, I—

LYN   She throws coffee at me.

She throws her coffee at me. Hot, scalding—a moccachino
yet—all over my skirt—which is why I really need that
dry—. So what do I do? I run to the parking lot. Little
does Ms. Fuck Head know, but I carry an extra skirt in
the back of the car. Fifteen years, I'm prepared for anything. So. I'm in the back seat, pulling off the moccachino
skirt—not going to change in the office, not going to
give her the pleasure—when I see it. I gotta run in my
hose. I gotta run looks like a, a, a varicose vein leaking
down my brand new hose. So there I am: no skirt, bare
legs, it's like five degrees, my naked ass is freezing to
the backseat, when I remember. I remember I always
carry an extra pair in my briefcase. Fifteen years, I'm
prepared for anything. I bolt into action: Pull off the old
skirt, pull off the old hose, pull on the new hose, pull on
the new skirt, wipe the coffee from my blouse—don't
have an extra blouse, but luckily I'm wearing the navy
blazer—check the mirror: lipstick, powder, a quick
brush of the hair, and I'm as good as new. In fact, I'm
better than new. Run across the parking lot, stroll in the
door, see Darlene, walk up to her, and look her in the
eye. And you know what I do? Know what I do?

Pause.

(triumphant) I. Do. Nothing.

She is beneath me. She is a floor below. Consummate
professional I am. Proceed as if nothing happened. And

do you think she says anything? Do you think she says a thing to me? Does she?

ANDY   I've been fired.

      Pause.

Twenty minutes to clear off my desk. Twenty minutes for ten years. Ten years.

      Pause.

LYN   Great. That's just great.

• • •

SAM   As we, as we see here, cells from a primary neoplasm become autonomous, undergoing a physical separation from the primary tumour, and invading other tissue. It's... it's as if the fidelity of the basement membrane is being challenged. You see?

• • •

      ANDY overlooking the lake. SAM watches him. She approaches.

SAM   Beautiful day.

      Pause.

ANDY   Yes.

SAM   The lake.

ANDY   Yes.

SAM   The trees.

ANDY   Yes.

SAM   The park.

ANDY   Mm.

      Pause.

SAM   I like it here.

ANDY   Yeah.

      Pause.

SAM Every day.

ANDY Hm?

SAM Every day I see you. Here. Sitting. Every day.

ANDY Yeah.

SAM Time off work?

ANDY Yeah. Uh, no. Not really, I....

> *Pause.*

Fired, downsized, whatever. Twenty minutes to clear off my desk. Twenty minutes for ten years. Ten years....

> *Pause.*

SAM Now you can enjoy it.

ANDY Being laid off?

SAM No silly. The park.

ANDY Ah. Right. The park.

> *He smiles. She smiles.*

SAM Do you mind if I...?

ANDY Of course not, I should have...

SAM I hope I'm...

ANDY No.

SAM 'Cause I don't want...

ANDY Not at all.

SAM I wouldn't want, you know, if you're...

ANDY Please.

> *She sits. Pause.*

You see. The problem is—with what you just said—the problem is: I loved my job.

SAM Really? Loved?

ANDY Yeah.

SAM   And what did you love?

ANDY   What did I...?

SAM   About your job.

ANDY   Well....

> *Pause.*

What I did.

SAM   Ah.

ANDY   What I was doing.

SAM   Uh huh.

ANDY   It was... fun. It was... challenging. It was... you know. The Government.

> *She laughs. He smiles.*

You?

SAM   I've never loved a job.

ANDY   No no, I meant...

SAM   Oh. I'm a, I'm a student. At the university.

ANDY   Ah. And you don't love that? What you're studying?

SAM   *(playful)* It's... fun, it's... challenging, it's... you know. The University.

> *They laugh. Pause.*

No, never loved anything.

> *She looks out.*

Except this day. I love this day.

ANDY   Never really thought about it. The "day." Always inside.

SAM   You see? What you've been missing?

ANDY   I suppose.

> *She closes her eyes, suns her face. He watches.*

So you come here...?

SAM   *(eyes closed)* Every day. Almost. Don't live far from here. I have a beautiful view of this park. Beautiful....

    She suns herself. He watches.

ANDY   And you, what, you come here and you...

SAM   I just... listen.

ANDY   Ah.

SAM   To the day. The time. The moment.

ANDY   The...?

SAM   The moment.

ANDY   I'm not sure...

SAM   Try it.

ANDY   What, you mean...?

SAM   Close your eyes.

ANDY   Close my...?

SAM   For a second.

ANDY   I don't know, I...

SAM   Go on. Trust me.

    Pause.

ANDY   All right.

    He closes his eyes.

SAM   Now just... listen.

ANDY   Okay.

SAM   *(slowly)* Imagine this day. See it in your mind. The sun on your face. The spring in your mouth. Your heart deep inside. No future. No past. No time. Just this day. This moment.

    She moves closer.

This is the moment. When everything changes. When the sun sets. When the leaves fall. When the ice melts.

When the air smells like sweet spring, or dying fall, or clean winter. When things change. Right now.

She is very close.

Open your eyes.

He does.

Well?

ANDY   ...wow.

SAM   Did that... scare you?

ANDY   I...

SAM   Excite you?

ANDY   That depends on...

SAM   Turn you on?

ANDY   Uh, yeah, I uh, yeah, sure. *(recovering)* You see, I loved my job—

SAM   Shhh.

Her finger to his lips.

Listen.

ANDY   I...

SAM   Listen.

ANDY   I'm not sure...

SAM   Look at me.

He looks at her.

ANDY   I don't...

SAM   Shhh.

She places his hand on her breast.

Do you hear it?

ANDY   Yes.

SAM   Do you?

ANDY Yes.

SAM Do you?

       Pause.

ANDY Yes.

       He kisses her. She responds.

• • •

SAM *(undressing)* Shhh.

ANDY She says, and the sound leaps from her tongue.

SAM Shhh.

ANDY She says. Music rises from the well of her throat, and I drink.

SAM *(teasing)* Be patient.

ANDY She says. And I, who am older; I, who am to be softer; I, who am to be wiser; I, who am to know all these things...

SAM *(giggles)* Be patient.

ANDY ...know nothing. And learn from her, to...

SAM Be patient.

ANDY To...

SAM Shhh.

ANDY To...

SAM Listen.

• • •

LYN Hi.

ANDY Hey.

LYN You're home.

ANDY Yeah.

LYN Christ what a day.

ANDY Oh?

LYN Goddamn bitch.

ANDY Who.

LYN Darlene.

ANDY Ah.

LYN Clean the bathroom?

ANDY Nope.

LYN Take out the garbage?

ANDY No.

LYN Lift a fucking finger?

> *Pause.*

I know, Andy.

ANDY *(nervous)* What?

LYN I know.

ANDY Know what.

LYN I know what you're going to say. "It's hard." Right?

ANDY *(relieved)* Ah. Well...

LYN It's hard when you don't have work. It's hard watching the walls, it's hard watching the dishes get dirty, it's hard watching the vacuum when it's turned on, it's hard watching the bills arrive, praying they'll pay themselves. It's so fucking hard. Maybe it's too much to ask. Maybe it's too much for you to either work at home, or get off your ass and—

ANDY I had an interview today.

> *Pause.*

As a matter of fact.

> *Pause.*

LYN Oh.

ANDY   Yeah.

LYN   And?

ANDY   Contract position. No pension, no medical.

LYN   And?

ANDY   A fraction of what I used to earn.

LYN   And?

ANDY   You really want to know?

LYN   Of course.

ANDY   Because it might be hard, it might be difficult—

LYN   Tell me!

ANDY   All right. All right.

        Pause.

        So I walk into the room, and there's these three... kids, how they got where they are I have no idea. Half my age, twice the attitude, three times the confidence.

LYN   Right.

ANDY   One's in jeans if you can believe it, the other two have nose rings, that's new to me, and they're like, you know, off some TV show, that one, you know, the one where, what's it called...?

LYN   Yeah yeah yeah.

ANDY   And so they sit me down, and get me a, a, you know, one of those coffees you always order.

LYN   A latte?

ANDY   Yeah. And they start on the basic questions: who are you, tell us about yourself, why'd you leave your last position, you know.

LYN   Uh huh.

ANDY   And I'm feeling pretty good, I'm calm, I'm answering the questions, I feel like we're, you know, connecting on some level, like I might make it through this, like I might get this thing, like I can handle it, you know?

LYN   Sure.

ANDY   But then. Then it gets really—then they start in with the real questions.

LYN   Like?

ANDY   They ask me about my skills in maximizing server uptime through practical and emerging management tools. They ask me if I'd feel comfortable heading up their e-commerce department. They ask me what considerations I'd take into account when setting up a cyber conference with seven stakeholders in seven different cities.

LYN   And?

ANDY   And?

LYN   What'd you say?

ANDY   What'd I—? I didn't know what the fuck they were *talking* about!

> *Pause.*

LYN   So?

ANDY   They might need someone in accounting. Accounting. Christ.

LYN   And?

ANDY   That was it. Showed me the door, nice meeting you, thanks for coming in, we'll get back to you.

LYN   "Get back to you?"

ANDY   Friday.

LYN   "Get back to you?"

ANDY   That's what they said.

LYN   "By Friday."

ANDY   Will you stop.

LYN   What.

ANDY   Stop it.

LYN   What!

ANDY   You're not being supportive.

LYN   You call that an interview?

ANDY   And what would you call it.

LYN   A blow-off, honey, that is what I call a fucking blow-off.

ANDY   Thanks, thanks a lot.

LYN   You have to be aggressive.

ANDY   Aggressive.

LYN   You've been in government too long.

ANDY   Have I.

LYN   You've got to learn to play the game.

ANDY   I know how to play the game.

LYN   Not out there you don't.

ANDY   I know.

LYN   Not out there.

ANDY   I KNOW.

> *Pause.*

> What do you want me to do? Huh? *Force* them to hire me? I'm trying. And you know what? It *is* hard. And I don't need you rubbing—I don't need you—I don't need you telling me—

LYN   I never said—

ANDY   It's not what you say, Lyn, it's the way you look.

LYN   The way I what?

ANDY   That look.

LYN   What—

ANDY   There.

LYN   Give me a fucking—

ANDY   That look.

LYN   This is ridic—

ANDY   There again.

LYN   Andy.

ANDY   And again. That look. You look at me like I'm worthless. Like I'm stupid.

LYN   Stop it!

ANDY   No you! You stop it! You stop it with your "you're so stupid, why the fuck did I marry you" look. You stop it.

> *Pause.*

That's what you're thinking. Isn't it? When you give me that look. Isn't it?

LYN   Andy.

ANDY   "…lousy husband, lousy lay…"

LYN   I never—

ANDY   Ah! But the look.

> *Pause.*

Uh?

> *Pause.*

You know it's true. You know it.

> *Pause. She opens her arms.*

LYN   Come here.

ANDY   Why.

LYN   I want to give you a hug.

ANDY   No.

LYN   Come here.

ANDY   No. You come over here and give me a hug if you want
       to give me a hug.

       She relents, comes to him. Hugs him.

LYN   Mmmmm.

ANDY   Mmmmm.

       *He responds, nibbles her neck, begins undressing her,
       making his way to her breast.*

LYN   ...Andy....

ANDY   Remember the time.

LYN   What....

ANDY   That time in the house.

LYN   What house?

ANDY   The show home.

LYN   Oh God.

ANDY   That big empty room.

LYN   That was years...

ANDY   The cool carpet.

LYN   My first sale.

ANDY   The fresh paint.

LYN   My first commission.

       He begins to make love to her.

ANDY   *(slowly)* And I laid you back. Back. 'Til we fell to the
       floor. The silence of new suburbs. And the windows,
       undressed. And the lights in the house. All of them. On.
       Burning. And we—

LYN   *(sharp pain)* AH!

ANDY   What.

LYN   Careful.

ANDY   What. What did I...?

LYN   They're not apples you know.

ANDY   I know!

>*Pause.*

I know.

>*Pause.*

Lyn. When are we—?

LYN   It's always the same.

ANDY   What?

LYN   It's predictable.

ANDY   Is it.

LYN   You think you know what I want.

ANDY   That's because we never do it. If we did it—

LYN   You never know what I want.

ANDY   You don't know what you want, how am I supposed to—

LYN   Fuck you.

ANDY   No, fuck you.

LYN   That's not true.

ANDY   It is. You can't make up your mind.

LYN   Maybe I have made up my mind.

ANDY   Oh, oh really.

LYN   Yeah.

ANDY   'Cause I'm just being "aggressive."

LYN   Maybe it's not you.

>*Pause.*

ANDY   Now what's that supposed to mean.

>*Pause.*

LYN   Maybe I'm not sure anymore.

ANDY   What if I said that to you.

LYN   Maybe it's not right.

ANDY   What if I said "maybe it's not you, Lyn."

LYN   Maybe we need something different.

ANDY   What if I said "I'm sleeping with someone else."

>   *Pause.*

LYN   Excuse me? I never said that.

ANDY   You, you know what I—

LYN   I never said that.

>   *Pause.*

>   What's going on.

>   *Pause.*

>   Andy.

ANDY   Nothing.

LYN   Are you...?

ANDY   What.

LYN   Are you...?

ANDY   What!

>   *Pause.*

LYN   *(incredulous)* Are you screwing someone?

>   *Pause.*

ANDY   What, you think I'm not capable of—

LYN   I didn't say—

ANDY   Because if that's what you—

LYN   What the hell is—?

ANDY   I just want things to be the way they were before.

LYN   They can't.

ANDY   I want to make things better.

LYN   You can't.

ANDY   I want things to be different then. I don't care. I just don't want this.

>   *Pause.*

LYN   It's sick, Andy. This marriage is ill.

ANDY   Then let's see someone.

LYN   We've been there.

ANDY   Someone new. I hear there's a good therapist—

LYN   It won't help.

ANDY   What if—if we had a baby.

LYN   Andy.

ANDY   So what then.

LYN   I don't know.

ANDY   What can I do, tell me.

LYN   I said I don't—

ANDY   WHAT.

LYN   *(fierce)* Nothing!

>   *Pause.*

>   Take out the garbage.

>   *Pause.*

>   And find a fucking job.

• • •

ANDY   I bite into her breast. Hard.

SAM   That's it.

ANDY   She says. I bite into her breast.

SAM   I like it like that.

ANDY I bite, testing her flesh, teasing her skin, tasting her fruit, until her mind shudders—

SAM That's it.

ANDY She says.

SAM *(orgasm)* That's it.

• • •

ANDY Thanks.

SAM Mmm.

ANDY That was great.

SAM Mmm.

They dress, slowly.

ANDY So.

SAM So.

ANDY When will I...? When will we...?

SAM *(smiles)* Whenever we meet.

ANDY Thursday.

SAM Whenever we meet.

ANDY Come on.

SAM I can see you from up here. From my window. I can see you when you walk into the park. When you sit on the bench. When you wait.

ANDY You like that don't you.

SAM What.

ANDY Watching me wait.

SAM Something about meeting outside.

ANDY Yes. But when.

SAM *(teasing)* You are impatient, aren't you. We'll have to work on that.

ANDY I need to know.

SAM   Whenever. Trust me.

ANDY   Thursday. Four o'clock.

       Pause.

SAM   I can't.

ANDY   Why not.

SAM   I thought we agreed—

ANDY   But don't you think—?

SAM   No pasts, no futures. Nothing. Just this. This moment. Remember? It's better this way.

ANDY   Experience talking?

SAM   Does it matter?

       Pause.

ANDY   Don't you, don't you ever want to feel loved?

SAM   *(laughs)* Oh God.

ANDY   Well don't you?

SAM   No.

ANDY   Don't you ever want to feel someone fall asleep in your arms.

SAM   No.

ANDY   Watch the morning sun dance on their face.

SAM   No.

ANDY   Taste their tears, see them smile, listen to—

SAM   No.

ANDY   Why?

SAM   Because.

ANDY   Why?

SAM   Because!

       She finishes dressing, quickly.

I see it all day, I don't need it in my spare time.

>   *Pause.*

ANDY   So.

SAM   So.

ANDY   Sex.

SAM   Yes.

ANDY   That's all.

SAM   Yes.

ANDY   That's it.

SAM   What else do you want?

ANDY   I don't know, I....

>   *Pause.*

SAM   I'm not your way out.

ANDY   I'm not looking for that.

SAM   Then what are you looking for?

ANDY   A way in.

>   *Pause.*

A second chance.

SAM   You think you're the only one?

ANDY   I don't know. Am I?

SAM   It's time for you to go.

ANDY   Am I?

SAM   Go.

ANDY   Am I?

SAM   Please.

ANDY   *(a discovery)* I am. Aren't I.

>   *Pause.*

Aren't I?

Pause.

I'm leaving my wife.

SAM   ...Jesus.

ANDY   Not for you, not because of this.

SAM   Why then.

ANDY   Because.

SAM   Why! Why are—?

ANDY   It's time. It's not right anymore.

SAM   For you.

ANDY   For both of us. It'll be a relief. Believe me.

> *Pause.*

Meet me Thursday.

SAM   *(tempted)* I can't, I....

ANDY   Meet me.

SAM   You're asking me to...

ANDY   I'm not asking anything. I'm not asking how old you are, or if you're married, or what you do during the day that makes you so sad. I'm not asking any of that. Just meet me. At the park. That's all.

> *Pause.*

Will you do that?

> *Pause.*

Will you?

• • •

SAM   Now what's interesting about what's happening here, is that it's completely normal. It may seem unnatural, but this tumourigenesis, this cascade of metastasis, this breakdown, is really the same process that allows almost all living things to grow: an apple; the heart; a breast....

• • •

SAM   Are you Darlene?

LYN   *(distracted)* No. I'm, I'm Evelyn. And you're... Samantha, right?

SAM   Sam's fine.

LYN   Sam. So sorry I'm late, I just, uh, I just ran from—

SAM   I thought they were sending over Darlene.

LYN   Oh no. Didn't they tell you?

SAM   Tell me....?

LYN   Darlene's ill.

SAM   Oh?

LYN   A little accident.

SAM   Oh no.

LYN   Hot coffee.

SAM   Ouch.

LYN   First degree burn.

SAM   God.

LYN   One of those freak things. You know.

SAM   Right.

LYN   So I'm taking her calls.

SAM   Right.

LYN   Help each other out. You'll find our office works like a team.

SAM   Right.

LYN   I'm so sorry I'm late, but—

SAM   That's all right.

            Pause.

LYN   So.

> *LYN waltzes in.*
>
> You're selling.

SAM   Thinking about it.

LYN   Very nice.

SAM   Thanks.

LYN   New hardwood?

SAM   Yeah.

LYN   Paint?

SAM   In the summer.

LYN   One bedroom?

SAM   Two. The other one's…

LYN   Nice size, this bedroom.

SAM   Mm.

LYN   Oh my God!

SAM   What.

LYN   This view!

SAM   You like it?

LYN   Gorgeous.

SAM   Isn't it?

LYN   Look at that: the park.

SAM   Yeah.

LYN   The lake.

SAM   Yeah.

LYN   The trees.

SAM   Mmm.

LYN   Like a picture. So pretty this time of year.

SAM   Yes.

> *She stares.*

LYN Isn't that, isn't that, that bench?

SAM What?

LYN The one by the lake.

SAM Ah. Yeah.

LYN I know that bench.

SAM Oh?

LYN Don't live far from here myself.

SAM Oh?

LYN I've sat on that bench. My, my husband and I used to go there quite often. When we were first married. Looks so small from up here. So lonely, so....

LYN stares out the window.

SAM So. What do you think?

LYN *(still staring)* Oh I love the park.

SAM No. Of the place I mean.

LYN Oh!

SAM Think it'll sell?

LYN Oh it'll sell all right. No doubt about that. It'll sell.

SAM Great.

LYN Now. I just need to ask you a few questions. Hope you don't mind.

SAM I... suppose not.

LYN Standard stuff. So I know.

SAM All right.

LYN Why are you moving.

SAM Well....

LYN Problems?

SAM You mean—?

LYN	With the condo. Any problems. You'll have to disclose it eventually, might as well tell me now.
SAM	Oh no, no. No problems.
LYN	Water?
SAM	Fine.
LYN	Heat?
SAM	Fine.
LYN	Foundation, pool, parkade—
SAM	Everything's fine that I know of.
LYN	(*smiles*) Nobody's after you?
SAM	Pardon?
LYN	Banks, creditors, collection agencies.
SAM	No. No problems there.
LYN	Working?
SAM	I'm a, a student.
LYN	(*suspicious*) Oh. In…?
SAM	Medicine.
LYN	(*pleased*) Ah! Good! If you'd have said philosophy or English or something….
SAM	Right.
LYN	So how are you managing the place?
SAM	…managing…?
LYN	Well you are a student, how are you—
SAM	It's my mother's.
LYN	Oh?
SAM	Yes.
LYN	And she's, she's what, she's renting—?
SAM	She's dead.

Pause.

She...

Pause.

She died.

Pause.

LYN   Oh.

SAM   Yeah.

Pause.

LYN   I'm, I'm sorry, I—

SAM   That's all right.

LYN   I didn't mean—

SAM   She left me the place...

LYN   Of course...

SAM   ...but I'm not really sure I want to, you know, live here...

LYN   Of course.

SAM   ...so I'm just checking to see what it's worth.

LYN   Of course, of course. I'm sorry, I just thought: "she's a student..."

SAM   Right.

LYN   "...and what's a student doing owning..."

SAM   Right.

LYN   "...and it doesn't look like anybody else really lives here, no boyfriend, no husband, no...."

SAM   Husband? *(laughs)*

LYN   *(laughs)* No?

SAM   Oh God no.

LYN   Me. It's been sixteen years.

SAM   Really?

LYN   Sixteen years.

SAM   Wow. I can't imagine.

LYN   Neither can I. Sometimes.

SAM   He in real estate as well?

LYN   Oh no. He, well, he was in government, but he's... he's been laid off.

SAM   Oh.

LYN   Twenty minutes to clear off his desk. Twenty minutes for ten years. Ten years.

SAM   Oh.

>   *Pause.*

>   *(a discovery)* Oh.

LYN   Sometimes I—and maybe you'll feel this one day— sometimes I look at him and I... I don't remember, I don't remember who he is, or....

SAM   Things change.

LYN   They do. But it happens so... you hardly notice, you don't see things coming, and then it happens, out of the blue, something you never expected, never thought about, never even considered... something pops, something twigs, and you... you....

>   *She feels ill.*

>   Do you, do you mind if I....

>   *She sits on the edge of the bed.*

SAM   Are you all right?

LYN   It's nothing.

SAM   Are you sure?

LYN   No no, I'm fine, really.

SAM   I'll get you some water.

She goes.

LYN   I've just been a little.... I'm just a little stressed.

SAM   *(off)* Right.

LYN   With my husband not working and... and our marriage, it's, it's not....

SAM   *(off)* Right.

LYN   *(to self)* And now I have to, I have to....

> *LYN weeps. SAM enters. Unsure, she hands LYN a tissue.*

SAM   Here.

LYN   Thanks.

> *LYN blows. SAM hands her the water.*

SAM   Take a sip.

LYN   Thank you. I didn't mean....

> *Sips.*

I'm not usually....

> *Sips.*

I'm so embarrassed.

SAM   Don't be. You should see someone. A doctor.

LYN   Yes, well, funny that. I just came.

SAM   What.

LYN   From the doctor.

SAM   Oh?

LYN   Yes.

> *Pause.*

Anyway....

> *She puts on her best face.*

You're selling.

SAM   Thinking about it.

LYN   Well, I have one rule.

SAM   All right.

LYN   If you go with me, you don't go with anyone else. We're in this together. A kind of marriage. If you agree to that, I'll be there for you. I'll work hard for you. I'll do anything to get you the best price for this place. If you don't, I won't. Plain and simple. All right?

>   *Pause.*

Okay?

>   *She holds out her hand.*

Agreed?

• • •

>   *LYN sitting in the park. ANDY enters. He sees LYN. He is about to leave.*

LYN   Hi.

ANDY   *(anxious)* Hey.

LYN   What are you…? You're here.

ANDY   Yeah.

>   *ANDY looks around.*

Christ what a day.

LYN   Oh?

ANDY   Goddamn interviews.

LYN   Ah.

ANDY   Same old, same old.

LYN   Yeah?

ANDY   Too old for new stuff. Too young to be a C.E.O.

LYN   Right.

>   *ANDY looks around.*

ANDY   I... I was looking for you this morning.

LYN   Oh?

ANDY   Thought we could talk. I dropped by the office, but they said you went home.

LYN   Yeah.

ANDY   So I went home. But you weren't there.

LYN   No.

ANDY   And so I... I thought I'd come here. To the park. Clear my, clear my mind, you know?

He looks around.

LYN   I wanted to talk to you too.

ANDY   Yeah?

LYN   I phoned home, but you weren't there.

ANDY   The interview.

LYN   And so I came home, but you weren't back. And so I thought I'd come here.

ANDY   Right.

LYN   Clear my mind, clear my thoughts. Like you.

Pause.

ANDY   Well.

Pause.

We, uh, we better get home.

LYN   I thought we were going to talk.

ANDY   Right. So we should get home. So we can—

LYN   Sit for a while.

ANDY   Don't you think it'd be better if we—?

LYN   Sit.

Pause.

Please.

He sits, reluctantly.

You remember...? Remember when you proposed?

ANDY   Proposed? Uh, sure, we...

LYN   Up in the mountains. A day like today. We made love on
that cliff. Sat naked overlooking the lake. The smell of
the wind, the pines all around, cut off from the world,
our own little paradise. Remember?

ANDY   Sure.

LYN   And you said: "I promise to take care of you, Lyn.
Forever."

ANDY   Lyn....

LYN   "I promise."

Pause.

I haven't been very nice to you lately. I know that.

Pause.

I haven't fulfilled my end of the bargain, I see that now.

Pause.

I haven't been much of a wife, or a friend, or even
a roommate for that matter.

Pause.

I'm sorry.

ANDY   Lyn, we've tried. We've tried. But we both know—

LYN   I have a job for you.

Pause.

ANDY   You have a job for me. You do.

LYN   Yes.

Pause.

I went to the doctor.

ANDY   Oh?

LYN   I've been feeling tired and...

ANDY   Are you...?

LYN   I...

ANDY   You're not—are you pregnant?

LYN   No. No....

ANDY   *(relieved)* No, no of course....

LYN   No. I've got a....

>   *Pause.*

In my breast.

>   *Pause.*

I'm going to need your help.

>   *Pause.*

That's your job. I need you to take care of me.

>   *SAM enters, unseen to ANDY and LYN. She*
>   *watches from a distance. As the lights fade, ANDY*
>   *steps forward, overlooking the lake.*

ANDY   I listen. But I hear nothing. Until she holds me. Hard.
And only then does my imagination shudder, and the
tears spill from her eyes, down my neck, to my breast,
to my own...

LYN   That's your job.

ANDY   She says.

LYN   To take care of me.

ACT TWO

*ANDY overlooking the lake. SAM watches him. LYN
in a different world, paring things down. (Please see
Production Notes on page 6.)*

ANDY   I stare at the lake.

LYN   "Poison."

ANDY   She says. I listen to the trees.

LYN   "Temptation."

ANDY   She says. I smell the fall air.

LYN   *(smiles)* "Opportunity."

ANDY   *(fondly)* She says. I look into her eyes. Not hard.
But gently. Scanning her thoughts, searching her mind,
surveying her trust. Until her mouth shivers, and
a smile slowly spills across her lips, her cheeks, her face,
spreading to my own eyes, to my own—

LYN   "Knowing."

ANDY   She says.

LYN   "It's about knowing."

• • •

SAM   Hello, I'm Samantha, Dr. Herbert asked me to look after
your file while she's—

LYN   Yes. She told me.

SAM   Oh.

    Pause.

    Oh my God, you're...

LYN   Lyn.

SAM   Of course. I didn't—

LYN   Make the connection.

SAM   The condo.

LYN   Overlooking the park, right?

SAM   Yes. Yes of course. So, so I'm guessing....

LYN   I'm on leave.

SAM   Right. Right.

        Pause.

        I'm Dr. Herbert's assistant. I'm a resident. I'm studying oncology.

LYN   Yes. Did you do it?

        Pause.

SAM   Do it?

LYN   Sell the condo.

SAM   Oh. No. Not yet. I got caught up in, in other things.

LYN   Have you seen my husband?

        Pause.

SAM   I'm, I'm sorry?

LYN   My husband.

        Pause.

SAM   I don't think...

LYN   He's supposed to be here.

SAM   Oh?

LYN   Don't know where he is. He's usually on time.

SAM   He's, he's coming here?

LYN   He sits in on my appointments.

SAM   I see.

LYN   All the goddamn questions you people ask.

SAM   If you...

LYN   I can never remember—

SAM   If you want...

LYN   The same questions, over and over—

SAM   We can always postpone—

LYN   Name, address, phone, occupation, pregnancies,
abortions, birth control, smoking, allergies, family
history, no, no, yes, yes, no, my auntie Jean, Christ!
Can't think straight anymore, can't—and that Dr.
Herbert—

SAM   Perhaps we should—

LYN   I have to tell you, that woman is a goddamn bitch.
I know one when I see one, and I'm telling you that Dr.
Herbert is one. And I know she's your boss, your super-
visor, whatever, but I'm telling you she's a bitch, and
she knows she's a bitch, 'cause when I first came to see
her, it was like, like….

> Pause.

She's feeling around me like I'm some piece of…. Makes
me go through all these tests, all these…. Here for
blood, there for X-rays. Meanwhile I miss closing a deal,
a good commission, been working on it for months, and
here I am running halfway across the city, not knowing
what I'm doing, not knowing what's going on, not
knowing….

> Pause.

And that afternoon, she calls me, she calls me, and she
says, "looks like we'll have to do a biopsy after all,"
she says, like I get this done every day, "looks like we'll
have to do a biopsy after all," like I'm getting my
fucking teeth cleaned. So I get the biopsy and that's,
well what can I say, no fun, and I get called into the
office, and I sit here, right here, and she says, standing
where you are, she says to me, with a straight face she
says: "You've got metaplastic adenosquamous cancer.
I recommend a mastectomy with Taxotere and if that
doesn't work, well there's really not much of a treatment regimen without cure, never mind a treatment regimen with cure," and I ask you, I ask you: What the
fuck does THAT mean?

> She is exhausted, but presses on.

And so I say to her "Dr. Herbert, does that mean I'm
going to die? Is that what you're telling me? That
I'm going to die?" And you know what she says to me?
Know what she says?

Pause.

"Some people see this as a gift. Maybe you should look
at it as a gift."

Pause.

And I said to her, I said: "Now listen to me, you
goddamn bitch. This is a disease. This is a curse. This
is poison. And don't you dare tell me... don't you dare
tell...."

LYN weeps.

SAM   We can do this later. All right, Lyn? We can....

ANDY enters.

ANDY   Sorry I'm late, I—

A long pause, as LYN weeps. Finally:

SAM   *(to ANDY)* I, I'm Samantha, I'm Dr. Herbert's—

ANDY   *(quietly)* Please leave.

Pause.

SAM   I only—

ANDY   Leave.

SAM   I'm only—

ANDY   Leave.

Pause.

Please.

SAM exits. ANDY goes to LYN.

LYN   ...I'm not...

ANDY   Shh.

LYN   ...I'm not feeling very...

ANDY   Shh. It's okay. We'll get you home. We'll get you home. Okay?

LYN   …It's not a gift, it's not….

ANDY   Shhh.

• • •

SAM   Here we can see cells growing in a relatively uncontrolled fashion, separating from one another to begin invasion. With time, the number of these cells will increase until they represent the majority. In this case here, the tumour resides in the breast of….

>   *Pause.*

A married female in her, her early- to mid-forties.

• • •

ANDY   *(dishevelled)* …Hello….

SAM   Well hello.

ANDY   Beau… beautiful day.

SAM   Yes.

ANDY   The lake.

SAM   Yes.

ANDY   The trees.

SAM   Yes.

ANDY   The park.

SAM   Mm.

>   *Pause.*

ANDY   Time off work?

SAM   Yeah. Uh, no, not really, I… taking a break.

>   *Pause.*

ANDY   Do you mind if I…?

SAM   No.

ANDY   I hope I'm...

SAM   No.

ANDY   I wouldn't want, you know, if you're—

SAM   Please.

He sits.

ANDY   *(sighs)* Oh boy oh boy oh boy oh boy oh boy.

Pause.

SAM   I'm sorry.

ANDY   Eh?

SAM   About what happened. I didn't know. Believe me, I had no idea.

ANDY   Yeah, well....

Pause.

SAM   Are you... have you been drinking?

ANDY   Yup.

SAM   Why.

ANDY   Why not.

Pause.

SAM   Have you... are you working?

ANDY   No. Yes, what am I saying. Full time, as a matter of fact.

SAM   Doing?

ANDY   What do you think.

SAM is silent.

Been doing a lot of listening.

Pause.

Listening to the leaves. Fall off the tree. In our yard. Quiet, so quiet, down to the ground, one by one. They let go. They just... let go. And I think, how hard can it be? How hard can it be to just....

> *Pause.*

There's this one. Big old apple. Sweetest bite you ever tasted. Perfect. But this year…. They fell hard. Not like the leaves. They fell hard. Just lay fallow on the ground. Birds wouldn't even touch 'em. Bitter, so bitter….

> *Pause.*

SAM   Every day, I look for you. Every day, I stare down from my window. To see if you've come. Every day.

> *Pause.*

ANDY   I have to tell her.

SAM   What?

ANDY   I need to, before—

SAM   You can't do that. Not now.

ANDY   I want—

SAM   Listen.

ANDY   I—

SAM   Listen—

ANDY   I have to do something!

> *Pause.*

Christ, how can I, how can I….

> *He weeps. She holds him.*

SAM   Shhh.

> *Pause.*

Come with me.

> *Pause.*

I can make you feel better, I can…

> *She doesn't say it.*

Just for today.

> *She kisses him. He responds.*

• • •

LYN	Andy...
	Andy...
	Andy....
ANDY	Oh...
LYN	Careful...
SAM	Yes....
ANDY	Oh God....
LYN	They're not...
SAM	Bite....
ANDY	Please....
LYN	*(quietly, in pain)* Andy....
SAM	Hard.
ANDY	What...?
SAM	Yes!
LYN	Help me!
ANDY	What is it?
SAM	Yes!
LYN	Help me!
ANDY	What is it?!
LYN	HELP ME!
SAM	*(orgasm)* Yes!
ANDY	*(wakes)* NO!!

       ANDY breathing hard.

SAM	What is it?

       Pause.

What. What is it?

       Pause.

What?

• • •

LYN   Hi.

ANDY   Hey.

LYN   You're home.

ANDY   Yeah.

LYN   Christ what a day.

ANDY   Oh?

LYN   That old chemo.

ANDY   Ah.

LYN   Flowers.

ANDY   Nice huh?

LYN   From who?

ANDY   Guess.

LYN   You.

ANDY   No.

LYN   Good. I hate these fucking things. It's like...

ANDY   Lyn....

LYN   It's like I'm already, like I'm already....

ANDY   They just want you to get better.

LYN   Yeah right.

ANDY   They don't know how to act, they don't know....

LYN   Yeah, yeah. Who are they from then?

ANDY   Guess.

LYN   I don't know.

ANDY   Guess.

LYN   ANDY!

ANDY   *(smiling)* Guess.

          She thinks. Then:

LYN	Fuck off.
ANDY	Yup.
LYN	No.
ANDY	Oh yes.
LYN	Darlene?
ANDY	Bingo.
LYN	Fuck off.
ANDY	Bingo!
LYN	Goddamn bitch. She's just feeling guilty.
ANDY	Lyn.
LYN	I'm serious. I mean how can she NOT feel guilty. The coffee...
ANDY	Honey.
LYN	...the clients she stole from me.
ANDY	*(laughs)* Stole from you!
LYN	Goddamn bitch!
ANDY	At least she bothered. You know how many people have called me since I left work?
LYN	None?
ANDY	Exactly. It's like I've died or something, like I've—

Pause.

(horrified) Oh God. I'm sorry.

But LYN laughs, in spite of herself.

I'm so sorry.

She laughs even louder and he joins in, embarrassed.

So.

LYN	Here we are.
ANDY	Another fun-filled Saturday night.

LYN   Clean the house?

ANDY   Yes.

LYN   Water the plants?

ANDY   Yes.

LYN   Take out the garbage?

ANDY   As a matter of fact I did.

LYN   Fuck you! Leaving me with nothing to complain about.

ANDY   Should I make a mess?

LYN   Yes.

ANDY   Fuck it up?

LYN   Yes.

ANDY   Give you something to be pissed off at?

LYN   Yes.

ANDY   Well then. I will: I saw a job listing.

LYN   Oh?

ANDY   Thought I might apply.

LYN   Really.

ANDY   Yup.

LYN   What a concept.

ANDY   Best to keep you on your toes.

LYN   What's it for.

ANDY   Really want to know?

LYN   Andy.

ANDY   You're sure now.

LYN   Tell me.

ANDY   'Cause it may be hard, it may be difficult—

LYN   *(laughs)* I'll kill you, I will.

ANDY All right, all right. Ready?

Pause.

Health Watch.

LYN Oh for Christ....

ANDY They need a bookkeeper.

LYN Andy.

ANDY What.

LYN Health Watch?

ANDY What.

LYN A not-for-profit?

ANDY And what's wrong with—?

LYN That's worse than government for God's sake. That's worse than retail.

ANDY *(smiles)* Gotta start somewhere.

LYN Health Watch! Christ.

ANDY Besides, it's a good cause.

LYN Ha!

ANDY Besides, we need the money.

LYN Do we?

ANDY Yeah.

Pause.

LYN Do we?

Pause.

ANDY Yeah. Yeah, we do.

Pause.

LYN Fuck. I'm sorry.

ANDY Don't be—

LYN This is my fault.

ANDY   Lyn, this is not your—

LYN   It is.

ANDY   Lyn—

LYN   FUCK THIS SHIT. FUCK IT.

Pause.

(fierce) Why is this happening. Tell me. What did I do that was so wrong. I never hurt anybody. Okay, so I threw coffee on Darlene, so I'm not a fucking SAINT, okay? But for Christ sake, is that any reason to do this? Is it?

ANDY   This has nothing to do with—

LYN   Look at me.

ANDY   Don't.

LYN   I used to be beautiful.

ANDY   You still are, don't—

LYN   Fucking liar. Look at me.

ANDY   Don't distance yourself from—

LYN   LOOK AT ME!

Pause.

I have no hair. My skin is the colour of… nothing. My blood is full of poison. And you dare tell me I'm beautiful. You dare look me straight in the goddamn face and tell me that I'm beautiful.

ANDY   Yes.

Pause.

Yes I do.

Pause.

Yes.

LYN   I never loved you.

ANDY   Don't be mean.

LYN   I never loved you.

ANDY   If you think this will make things easier—

LYN   I. Never. Loved. You.

ANDY   What about now?

LYN   What about now.

ANDY   Do you love me now?

> *Pause.*

LYN   Yes.

ANDY   Well that's a relief.

LYN   But I didn't before.

ANDY   That's okay.

LYN   *(sulking)* Only now because you're being nice to me.

ANDY   I don't care about before. As long as you love me now.

> *Pause.*

Well. I should go pick up some groceries.

LYN   I'll come with you.

ANDY   You certainly will not.

LYN   Samantha told me—

ANDY   You need to rest.

LYN   I need to follow a normal routine.

ANDY   Hey hey, I'm Mr. Caregiver, remember?

LYN   Samantha told me—

ANDY   I don't care!

> *Pause.*

LYN   What's with you.

ANDY   Nothing.

LYN   She's my—

ANDY I just think…

       Pause.

LYN What?

ANDY We don't have to listen to everything she says.

       Pause.

       That's all.

• • •

SAM Hi.

LYN Hi.

SAM Hello.

ANDY Hello.

       Pause.

SAM Well. I'm sorry to say this, but we're going to have to run more tests. We thought everything was in order, but….

ANDY What.

SAM There's some evidence the cells have metastasized—

ANDY What?

SAM The cancer cells, they metastasize, they—

ANDY What are you talking about?

LYN Andy.

SAM If you'd let me finish, I'd—

ANDY No.

LYN Andy.

ANDY I want to know what's going on in a language I understand.

SAM The cells grow quickly, they divide, they grow, they invade, and the whole thing repeats itself. We want to make sure there aren't any cancerous cells left. That's all.

Pause.

LYN   When do I....?

SAM   This afternoon.

LYN   Do I need to stay?

SAM   No, no. You can go home right after.

Pause.

If you have any other questions, please—

ANDY   No questions. We'll be back after—

LYN   What about sex.

Pause.

SAM   I beg your....?

LYN   Can my husband and I have sex.

ANDY   Lyn, I don't think—

LYN   I've been meaning to ask this for a while. Up until now we haven't, we just assumed, you know, that we shouldn't.

ANDY   Honey, is this really the—

SAM   Some women report that after surgery, when things have healed, their sex life returns to normal and in some cases, improves.

LYN   Really.

SAM   Yes.

LYN   Andy, did you hear that, some women report—

ANDY   I think it's time—

SAM   *(to LYN)* If you want to talk about—

ANDY   She doesn't need to—

SAM   I wasn't talking to you, I was—

ANDY   I think I know—

SAM   This isn't about you. All right?

> *Pause.*

LYN   Andy, why don't you go get the car.

> *Pause.*

ANDY   Lyn—

LYN   There's a few more things I'd like to discuss.

ANDY   I was hoping that—

LYN   Andy. Get the car.

> *Pause. He leaves.*

I'm sorry.

SAM   That's all right.

LYN   He's been under a lot of stress.

SAM   I understand.

LYN   He lost his job and...

SAM   Yes, you mentioned.

LYN   And then I got sick.

SAM   Right.

LYN   And for a while there, I even thought....

> *Pause.*

SAM   Thought what.

> *Pause.*

LYN   For a while there I thought....

> *Pause.*

He might be having an affair.

> *Pause.*

SAM   Oh?

LYN   Yes.

> *Long pause. They stare at each other.*

But it doesn't matter now.

SAM   Doesn't it?

LYN   No.

> *Pause.*

I don't know.

> *Pause.*

From what you said earlier, I take it it's spreading.

SAM   We don't know that, we have to—

LYN   Your educated guess. Please.

> *Pause.*

SAM   I'm worried it's spread to your, to your lungs.

> *Pause.*

LYN   I see. That's not good is it.

SAM   No.

> *Pause.*

LYN   Don't tell my husband.

SAM   Tell him what.

LYN   Anything.

SAM   Lyn, I...

LYN   If I want to tell him, I will.

SAM   I...

LYN   It doesn't matter. All right?

> *Pause.*

Okay?

> *She holds out her hand.*

Agreed?

• • •

ANDY   Oh God....

SAM	These cells…
LYN	Oh yeah….
SAM	…these "forces…"
ANDY	Jesus.
SAM	…keep growing…
LYN	Yes…. Yes….
SAM	…separating from one another…
LYN	That's it….
SAM	…invading… growing… separating…
LYN	That's it….
SAM	…invading… growing… until…
LYN	*(orgasm)* Yes…

> *Pause.*

SAM	…things break down. They… break down.

> *Pause.*

ANDY	Wow.
LYN	That was….
ANDY	When was the last time….?
LYN	Too long.
ANDY	Too fucking long.
SAM	…In this case, the metastasized cells have spread to the lungs and also to the brain.

• • •

ANDY	*(fierce)* Why didn't you tell me!
SAM	Because.
ANDY	Why!
SAM	She's my patient. Not you.

ANDY You should have told me first. I should have been the one to tell her.

SAM She didn't want that.

ANDY You should have told us together.

SAM I did what I thought was right.

Pause.

ANDY I can't....

Pause.

SAM What.

ANDY I can't do this anymore.

SAM · Listen.

ANDY Not now. Not now, I can't.

SAM I know it's hard, I know, but...

ANDY I can't, I can't, I can't.

Pause.

SAM All right.

Pause.

I understand.

ANDY Do you?

SAM If you can't, if it's not right, then I guess....

Pause.

ANDY All right.

Pause.

All right.

Pause.

Well then.

Starts to leave.

SAM Andy.

He stops. Turns to her.

When will we....?

Pause.

Couldn't we just....?

Pause.

I need to know if....

Pause.

ANDY   Look—

SAM   I need to know if—

ANDY   I thought we agreed—

SAM   I—

ANDY   What!

Pause.

SAM   I love you.

Pause.

ANDY   Wha....? Why didn't you—!?

SAM   Because. Because I...

Pause.

I've never been... I never felt... I've never said it. Not really. Not even to my—

ANDY   I asked you, I wanted you—

SAM   I know—

ANDY   And now, now you—

SAM   I know, you think I don't fucking—?!

ANDY   It's too late, it's, it's—.

SAM   Don't you dare, don't you DARE tell me it's too late, don't you—!

Pause.

I know when it's too late. I know.

Pause.

People die, Andy, you know that? People close to you, they die. And after it's over, you think "I never said it." I never said the words, I never told her I....

Pause.

But then it's too late, it's....

Pause.

And all you're left with is this hole, this.... And I worry. Worry it'll never get smaller. That it won't heal.

Pause.

So you stop saying it, because whenever you do, it's "too late" and before you know it, you, you forget, you know? You forget what it's like to say it, to say "I love you," forget what it means, forget....

Pause.

So I'm telling you now, Andy. I'm telling you I love you now so....

Pause.

So I don't forget.

Pause.

So I remember.

Pause.

You. That day. Sitting, staring at the lake. And I thought, looking at you, talking to you, kissing you, I thought, "maybe." Maybe here's someone who can, who....

Pause.

Who can heal me. Who could....

She weeps. He goes to her.

ANDY *(gently)* Shhh.

Pause.

SAM   Do you love her, Andy?

Pause.

Do you?

ANDY   I, I'm sorry, I....

SAM   Do you?

Pause.

ANDY   Yes. Yes I do.

SAM   Okay....

Pause.

Okay.

• • •

ANDY   Beautiful day.

LYN   *(weakened)* Yes.

ANDY   Don't you think?

LYN   Yes.

ANDY   The trees. The lake. The air.

LYN   Mm.

She coughs.

ANDY   When you get, when you get better, we'll, we'll come here more often. Once a week at least.

Pause.

Lyn? How come—

LYN   *(quietly)* Shh.

Pause.

Listen.

Pause.

Hear that?

ANDY   Mm.

>   *Pause.*

LYN   Come here. Come sit beside me. Come.

>   *He does.*

There's a few things we need to talk about.

ANDY   ...all right....

LYN   That I need to tell you.

ANDY   We shouldn't stay out too—

LYN   Shhh. Now listen. Listen to me. To what I'm saying.

>   *Pause.*

First. I want it to be simple.

ANDY   What do you mean?

LYN   You know what I mean.

ANDY   I...

LYN   You know what I mean.

ANDY   I...

LYN   You know.

>   *Pause.*

ANDY   I don't think we should talk about this.

LYN   Andy.

ANDY   It won't help.

LYN   Andy.

ANDY   You have to save your energy.

LYN   We have to. We have to plan.

ANDY   I don't want to plan. Why do we have to plan? Who says we have to have a plan?

LYN   It'll make things easier. For later.

ANDY   To hell with later, to hell with the future, to hell with it. I care about this moment. This day. Right now.

LYN   And this is it. This is the moment. Where we talk about it.

> *Pause.*

I have to say this. Do you understand?

> *Pause.*

Do you understand, Andy?

> *He nods.*

We need a will.

ANDY   ...Jesus....

LYN   Listen. We need a will. We need one. I want you to call a lawyer. Get someone to come over this week. I'm giving you everything, but we need to make it official. Can you do that?

> *ANDY nods.*

Now: If—when—the time comes, you call my parents first. You call them first. Then yours. And you tell them to make the rest of the calls. Not you. Got that?

> *ANDY nods.*

Next. I want you—if you want to—I want you... I want you to feel free to, to marry again.

> *ANDY shakes his head.*

I know it's hard right now, to think about that, but... you can't let this poison your future. If an opportunity comes around, if you get a second chance, don't be, don't be, I don't know.... Just don't be a fucking moron.

> *He looks at her.*

ANDY   And how am I supposed to know if the "right opportunity" comes around?

LYN   If it's right, you'll know.

ANDY   I don't think so.

LYN   You will. It's all about knowing.

> *Pause.*

ANDY   You remember when I proposed? Remember?

LYN   Up in the mountains.

ANDY   A day like today. And the trees were, they were like a, a witness. Remember? And the air was, it was like a confirmation, it was so clean, so.... And we sat on the edge of that cliff, our legs dangling over the edge, staring down at that lake, like a, a crystal ball, squinting into our future. And I said, I said...

LYN   "I promise to take care of you."

ANDY   "Forever." I said "Forever."

> *Pause.*

Lyn, I have to tell you something.

LYN   Is this a regret?

ANDY   I need to—

LYN   Is it?

ANDY   Kind of.

LYN   'Cause I hate fucking regrets.

> *Pause.*

ANDY   I'm rotten you see.

> *Pause.*

To the core.

> *Pause.*

I tried before, but then you got sick, and I didn't, I didn't—

LYN   Andy.

> *Pause.*

I know.

Pause.

ANDY   I, I just wanted to say… I'm sorry.

LYN   I know.

She puts his hand to her heart.

I don't care about "before." I care about now. Okay?

He nods.

One more thing.

ANDY   What's that.

LYN   I want to be cremated.

ANDY   Oh for Christ…

LYN   I'm serious.

ANDY   All right. All right. Fine. Cremated. Fine. Whatever. And if I die before you, which I probably will—

LYN   Andy.

ANDY   —I want you to bury me. Put me down six feet under, so I know on judgment day, I can still crawl up from the muck, and prove to the fucking world I existed. All right?

LYN   Deal.

ANDY   And what, pray tell, am I supposed to do with the ashes.

LYN   Scatter them.

ANDY   Where?

LYN   On the lake.

ANDY   In the mountains?

LYN   No. Here. Right here.

ANDY   On this lake?

LYN   Yes.

ANDY   Isn't that illegal?

LYN   As if I care.

> *They laugh.*

As if I fucking care.

• • •

SAM   The prognosis for this patient is poor. About ninety per cent of these cases, these patients, these....

> *Pause.*

The chances are, this... woman is going to die very soon. But. Prevention, early detection, new treatments. That's where we come in. That's why we're here.

• • •

> *LYN barely conscious, her breathing laboured. ANDY, dozing.*

LYN   *(very weak)* ...cold....

ANDY   *(waking)* Wha...? Did you say...?

LYN   ...cold....

ANDY   Well. We'll just have to warm you up then.

> *Places his body, or a blanket, around her.*

How's that?

LYN   ...mmm....

ANDY   Good.

> *Pause.*

Lyn?

> *Pause.*

I want to tell you....

LYN   ...hm....

ANDY   I want to say..

> *Pause.*

I love you.

> *Pause.*

You know that?

> *Pause.*

I love you more than anything.

LYN   Shh...

> *He listens.*

(*dying*) Shh......

ANDY   She says. Until her mind shudders. And the last of her breath spills into my ear, down my neck, to my breast, to my own....

LYN   Shhhh......

• • •

> *The season changes. ANDY overlooking the lake. SAM watches him. She approaches.*

SAM   Hello.

> *Pause.*

Beautiful day.

> *Pause.*

The lake, the trees, the....

ANDY   (*smiles*) Yes.

> *Pause.*

SAM   I'm sorry.

ANDY   Yeah well. Been six months.

SAM   Time passes slowly.

ANDY   Yeah.

> *Pause.*

SAM   Do you mind if I...? I hope I'm, I mean I don't—

ANDY   Please.

>   *She sits. They look out.*

SAM   Every day. Every day you come. Stare out at the lake. Every day.

>   *Pause.*

I would have come earlier....

ANDY   No.

SAM   But I didn't think....

ANDY   No. That was right. What you did.

>   *Pause.*

SAM   Is there anything I can do?

ANDY   ...no.

SAM   Sure?

ANDY   Yeah.

SAM   You don't, you don't need anything?

ANDY   A new job.

>   *He smiles.*

SAM   Is that all?

>   *She slides her hand over to his.*

ANDY   I....

>   *He gently takes her hand. Cups it in his own.*

SAM   I understand.

ANDY   Do you?

>   *Pause.*

SAM   Yes. I do. This is the moment, right? *(smiles)* When everything changes.

>   *Pause.*

ANDY   Thank you.

Pause.

SAM   I'll still watch you, you know. From my window.

ANDY   I'd like that.

She turns to leave.

SAM   'Bye.

ANDY   'Bye. Samantha.

She smiles and slowly walks away. ANDY stands, overlooking the lake. LYN in a different world.

I stare out over the lake.

LYN   Goodbye.

ANDY   She says. I stare out over the lake. Not hard. But gently. Scanning her memory, searching her face, surveying her smile. Until my mind....

And the hint of a smile spills across his lips, his cheeks, spreading to his eyes.

LYN   Goodbye.

ANDY   She says.

LYN   Goodbye.

Pause.

ANDY   Goodbye.

He says, as the lights gently fade.

The end.

Blowfish

Is this what it's like, I thought then, and think now: a little blood here, a chomp there, and still we live, trampling the grass? Must everything whole be nibbled? Here was a new light on the intricate texture of things in the world, the actual plot of the present moment in time after the fall: the way we the living are nibbled and are nibbling—not held aloft on a cloud in the air, but bumbling and scarred, and broken, through a beautiful land.

—Annie Dillard
Pilgrim at Tinker Creek

I can only perceive a succession of cruel splendours whose very movement requires that I die: this death is only the exploding consumption of all that was, the joy of existence of all that comes into the world; even my own life demands that everything that exists, everywhere, ceaselessly give itself and be annihilated…. I imagine myself covered with blood, broken but transfigured, and in agreement with the world….

—Georges Bataille
Heraclitean Meditation from Vision of Success

Unable to do anything. Unable to act. The body is a dead land…. If the world in which you live is sick, you have to live in the imaginary.

—Kathy Acker
In Memorium to Identity

to Eden, for her patience

Acknowledgements

The playwright gratefully acknowledges the following individuals and organizations: Mark Wilson, John Murrell, Eden Philp, the Saskatchewan Playwrights Centre, Alberta Theatre Projects, the Alberta Foundation for the Arts, Sage Hill Writing Experience, Lakeland College, Patti Sheddon, Tom Rooney, Catherine Rock, Bob White, Micheline Chevrier, David Mann, Greg Nelson, Raul Tome, Michael Spencer-Davis, John Farewell, Denise Kenney, Myrna Wyatt-Selkirk, Bonnie Green, Gil Osborne, Lindsay Bell, Marlene Klassen, Workshop West Theatre, Northern Light Theatre, the National Arts Centre, John Kirkpatrick, Christine Hanson, Adam Blocka, David Chapman, Nicola Devine, Emily Dykes, Kirsten Kilburn, Becca Murtha, Trina Pozzolo, Ian Rowe, Bretta Gerecke, Jim Reynolds, Susan Hayes, Heather Jopling, Tom Nerling, David Skelton, Aaron Bushkowsky, Conni Massing, Ann St. James, Kit Brennan, Ken Williams, Jerry Morrison, Michael Nathanson, Andrew Willmer, Carrie Thiel, Patrick Howarth, Julia Hoover, Matt Baram, Dion Johnstone, Tara Hughes, Leo Vernik, Yashoda Ranganatham, Alec McClure, Gregor Trpin, Victoria Rideout, and the University of Alberta Department of Drama.

And a special thanks to DD Kugler.

Blowfish was commissioned by Workshop West Theatre in 1995. It was subsequently given public workshops at: Workshop West's Springboards Festival, in February 1996; Alberta Theatre Projects' playRites Festival, in March 1996; and the Saskatchewan Playwrights Centre's Spring Festival of New Plays, in May 1996.

Blowfish was further developed and co-produced by Northern Light Theatre (Edmonton) and the National Arts Centre (Ottawa). It opened November 6, 1996 at Commerce Place (Edmonton), with the following company:

LUMIERE   John Kirkpatrick
CELLIST   Christine Hanson
ASSISTANTS   Adam Blocka, David Chapman
                  Nicola Devine, Emily Dykes
                  Kirsten Kilburn, Becca Murtha
                  Trina Pozzolo, Ian Rowe

Directed by DD Kugler
Designed by Bretta Gerecke
Stage Manager: Susan Hayes
Catering: Gourmet Goodies

• • •

Blowfish transferred to the Studio Theatre of the National Arts Centre (Ottawa) on November 28, 1996, with the following company:

LUMIERE   John Kirkpatrick
CELLIST   Christine Hanson
ASSISTANTS   Heather Jopling, Susan Hayes

Directed by DD Kugler
Designed by Bretta Gerecke
Stage Manager: Susan Hayes
Catering: Chef Kurt Waldele and the NAC catering staff
Studio Chief: Jim Reynolds

Characters

LUMIERE
ASSISTANTS

In the original production, LUMIERE played all of the following incidental characters. The assistants may appear as these characters, but preferably only as shadows of LUMIERE's memory and not in any naturalistic way.

BRIAN MULRONEY
MILA MULRONEY
MOM
FLETCHER
TROOPER
GUARD
WAITRESS
GREEKS
SECRETARY
VOICE

Production Notes

Blowfish runs approximately eighty minutes, which does not include the intermission where the meal is served.

Blowfish was originally performed using live music and real food. It is highly recommended that producers include some form of food, be it a buffet, a sit-down meal, or munchies. Music and/or sound also play a crucial role in this play. As in the original production, live music/sound may be used to set the play's mood; entertain the audience during intermission; establish leitmotifs for various characters, stories, and time periods; or inspire images of weather that appear frequently throughout the play.

ACT ONE

*A room. A long table with food. Large knives. A musician
plays. Perhaps various screens that project images. The
mood is charmed elegance, calculated opulence, precise
lushness. As LUMIERE greets his guests, he treats
them to an assortment of beverages and hors d'oeuvres.
LUMIERE, a man in his mid-thirties, is dressed impec-
cably. Nevertheless, his demeanour is edgy and a bit
ragged. He leads the catering, along with numerous
ASSISTANTS. When people have had time to settle,
LUMIERE begins.*

LUMIERE   Hello. And thank you for coming.

My name is Lumiere. I am a caterer, and what I have
for you tonight is a fête, a special event. I've requested
your presence here this evening—and you have been
so good as to oblige—for a variety of reasons. Number
one: to eat. As much as you like. We have victuals to
meet your every dining desire; we have foodstuffs
to tantalize your discerning palate; we have edibles
that will nourish your mind, as well as your soul; we
have it all. Number two: to listen. To me. Tell a few
stories, nothing too dull or overly long, I promise.
Just a few anecdotes to help you digest and, hopefully,
in the process, entertain and… enlighten you.
Number three: to observe, to witness, to….

But more on that later. Until then, rest, relax, and be
assured that throughout this evening's event, I am
here to serve you—my esteemed guests.

Let me tell you a story.

Thunder threatens in the distance.

• • •

LUMIERE   The brand new 1979 Ford barrels down Highway 3,
and turns off onto a dirt road. Gravel and dust fly.

The driver is not speeding.

He is sixteen years old, and this is his first day
driving by himself after acquiring his Alberta driver's
licence.

He is not stoned.
He is not drunk.
He is not careless.

His parents are loving and encouraging, but do not
spoil him. He makes his own lunches. He does his
own homework. Occasionally he masturbates. But he
always cleans up afterwards, and is fully cognizant
of its moral implications and biological purpose. He
mows the lawn Saturdays. He plays ball with his…
brother.

He goes for his driver's licence as soon as he turns
sixteen. And—like most teenagers—as soon as he
receives it, he goes to his father and asks him for the
keys, who, after a number of questions and warnings,
gives the keys to his son, who happily—but not
deliriously—starts the engine.

A taste of freedom. The brink of adulthood. His
whole life before him.

The brand new 1979 Ford barrels down Highway 3,
and turns off onto a dirt road. Gravel and dust fly.

Thunder threatens.

The clouds brew all day long in the western sky.
Now, in the early evening, a swirling storm boils onto
the dirt-and-gravel road. Hail splatters the windshield of the 1979 Ford, making the teen's visibility
less than desirable. A cold coil of wind sends the
brand new Ford twisting and turning on the wet
road.

The teen does not panic. He brakes normally.
Cold rain. Loose gravel. A deep ditch. Metal and
fibreglass fly.
A piece of the Ford's frame,
Through the windshield,

Through the nose,
To the brain.

Pause.

The teen never speaks intelligibly again. He cannot
communicate, he cannot walk unaided, and his nose
runs endlessly. The family wonders who is responsible
for this—God? or Fate? or Ford?

Later, the teen's brother and the teen's parents send
him to an institution, where everyone who visits the
teen (now a man) takes him to be defective from
birth, or crazy, or both.

He will... die.

Eventually.

Would anyone like some more?

• • •

The ASSISTANTS attend to people as needed.

LUMIERE   As I said, my name is Lumiere, and I am a caterer.
I might remind you at this time that caterers are not
chefs, although like chefs we prepare a great deal of
the meal. Unlike chefs, caterers do not indulge themselves in the food. We are rarely overweight. We don't
wear tall hats. We do not taste the soup and say "a little more salt." We rarely have fits of anger, and never
throw dishes at our serving staff, as do chefs. We
forgo ego.

Unlike chefs, my most important role is not to create
the food, but to serve the food. To you. To make the
most mundane hors d'oeuvre exciting, and the most
exotic seem irresistible. To ensure the napkin is
properly folded, the soup spoon precisely placed, the
room lovingly lit to match the desired atmosphere
and mood. The smallest detail must be perfect.
Timing is everything.

For the caterer, food is only the medium. My calling is
to create ceremony, to realize ritual.

A birthday party, for example, demands not only a cake, but the perfect cake that—along with specifically chosen candles and carefully selected liqueurs—creates an atmosphere of friendly fun, savoury celebration, a yearning for youth, and acceptable indulgence. Wedding receptions require an illusion of intimacy: bouquets of benevolence, lighting, sublime spirits, a miraculous meal, an atmosphere heavy with hope.

Funerals? Well!

A number of ASSISTANTS equipped with nail files, clippers, and pumice stones begin to give LUMIERE a manicure.

Food is comforting, and after a long day of weeping and keening, eating a sandwich brings much-needed relief and nourishment to the grieving body. Whether the funeral is a sombre service for a solitary stranger, or a spectacular soiree for a celebrated socialite, a few rudimentary rules are essential:

Nothing gooey, nothing gaudy. Nothing bitter, nothing bony. Nothing too hard to chew, too hard to digest, too much like the human body, like human flesh, like—

Well, you get my drift.

He inspects his nails.

(to ASSISTANTS) Thank you. *(They leave.)*

I confess it: I am fascinated by food and distracted by death.

• • •

LUMIERE   There are, after all, only four things in this world that link us as human beings:

Number one: Food. We all have to eat.
Number two: Death. We all have to die.
Number three: The Weather....

A fulmination.

And number four: Politics.

Without weather, we have no food. Without food, we have death. And the common thing about food, death, and the weather, is that we have no control over any of them. Let's face it, if you had to go out and sow an acre of oats, you wouldn't know where to begin. You wouldn't know how to forecast a storm if a wavering barometer stared you in the face. And you certainly wouldn't know how to bury a dead person, now would you?

Would you?

Politics is people. People like you and me. People converging in groups: families, churches, governments, unions, and political parties. The farmer, the weatherman, the undertaker. We give those people the unthankful job of trying to control things that are, for the most part, uncontrollable. Politicians, on the other hand, have been given the task of serving the public's hope that some things in life actually may be controllable: terrorism, unemployment, specialty channels, assisted suicide....

• • •

LUMIERE My parents were the kind of people who religiously voted—against the trend. If the Grits got in, they voted Conservative. If the Tories were strong, they voted NDP. And part of this Canadian electoral rite was to attend a campaign rally, in which my mother would inevitably embarrass everyone involved by holding up ME AND MY BROTHER as an example of everything that had gone wrong in the country. We were "the children whose parents couldn't afford to buy them a ball glove," or "the boys whose parents had to pay too much tax."

Mom knew how to work these things. She would descend on the candidate, and ask pointed questions; camera bulbs would flash, the candidate's lackey would scribble down my parent's name, and

eventually ball gloves would arrive in the mail, or
banks would call with new scholarship schemes.

And so it happened that in 1984 I graduated from
university and—surprise, surprise—I didn't have
a job. My dad was at a funeral and my brother was not
around, when my mother took me to a Progressive
Conservative rally. Not to support them, but to con-
front them. After all, Brian Mulroney himself would
be there.

My mother put on the practical, no-nonsense pantsuit she always wore to these events. We went to the
barbecue and waited for the appropriate cue, which
came after the speeches, just when the press started to
scrum.

Mulroney got up, and for the first time in my life,
I couldn't take my eyes off the podium. Standing
beside him was the most stunning creature I had ever
laid eyes upon. I'll never forget the warm, fall day
I first saw her.

Mila....

She was finishing a homemade hors d'oeuvre:
a simple cracker, cheddar cheese, and half-cherry
tomato, with a toothpick. But she lifted it to her lips
like it was the finest Russian caviar, like an oyster
freshly culled from the warmest, deepest waters.
Young, vivacious, friendly, sleek as an otter, legs for
days, speaks five languages, beautiful sweater with
ruby necklace and matching earrings, cool Jackie O.
sunglasses....

I could have devoured her.

BRIAN   Uh, Mila and I have been campaigning together for
           sixteen hours every day, and we're going to keep it
           up seven days a week if you'll promise to send—

LUMIERE   Whoever to Ottawa. As the applause began, Brian
           and Mila stepped off the podium into the scrum of
           reporters. My mother elbowed me out of my reverie,

	and headed through the crowd like a salmon heads upstream to deliver the precious egg.
MOM	*(bellows)* Excuse me, excuse me, Mr. Mulroney!
BRIAN	Uh, Yes?
MOM	I want to know why my son here can't find a job after three years of university training.
LUMIERE	My mother failed to understand that a BA doesn't get anyone a job, and certainly not when your degree is in philosophy.
BRIAN	*(hesitating)* Well....
MILA	What's your name?
LUMIERE	That voice. Like a fine claret: smooth, sweet, with a firm finish.
MILA	What's your name?
LUMIERE	She looked at me, and she knew. She knew I was mortified. She took me out of the scrum and pulled me to the side, as my mother battled it out with Brian and his assistants.
MILA	It must be very difficult for someone your age, especially when John Turner drops Celine Hervieux-Payette from the Liberal cabinet. I mean, she's the Youth Minister.
LUMIERE	I didn't hear much else. I only smelled her soul, revelled in her rays, felt her healing touch. She took down my name and promised to send me the Conservative Party plan on grants and tax credits for youth employment. Which I later received, along with a photo of her and Brian. On the back of the photo she wrote:
MILA	"Serve others, and others will serve you."
LUMIERE	I had the photo enlarged, then I cut out Brian, and hung Mila up on my wall. The smaller photo with the note I kept in my pocket for a long time, right up until....

Pause.

That chance encounter changed my life.

I was lazy, living at home, and had a philosophy degree. I didn't know what I wanted, I didn't know what I believed in, I had no… vision.

But after meeting Mila, I became a Young Conservative: independent, ambitious, responsible, debt-free, entrepreneurial, driven. I left home, moved to the city, and got a job as a security guard in a mall. Being in a mall landed me a job in a pet shop, selling weasels, where I met a man who spent his summers killing rats on the Alberta / Saskatchewan border (Alberta prides itself on being a "rat free" province). I spent the summer poisoning rats, which landed me in Medicine Hat, where I ended up writing instruction manuals for new pesticide-application devices, which led to various freelance writing jobs in Calgary, where I became, for a time, the person who wrote press releases for an organization called Canadians For a Better Canada, whose more radical members were accused of beating a man into unconsciousness. The man recovered, the radicals were convicted, and I was out of a job.

But. My work with Canadians For a Better Canada had put me in contact with a number of groups in Ohio, Oklahoma, and Texas. And so it happened that I ended up in that part of the world known broadly as "America's Breadbasket."

A lamenting wind.

• • •

LUMIERE The first time I met Robert Fletcher was in a corn field in Ohio. He was from the Three Hills area of Alberta, but spent a lot of his time in the States. People who knew Fletcher called him The Prophet.

FLETCHER See that?

LUMIERE Says Fletcher.

FLETCHER Have yourself a good look.

LUMIERE He points to a section of rotten, flattened corn crops.

FLETCHER That's what I mean. That's what we're trying to stop.

LUMIERE I stare at the wilting maize.

The Hopi Indians believed that corn was divinely granted to humanity as the Staff of Life. They dug deep pits in Mother Earth to store the consecrated cornmeal alongside their dead.

We retire to Fletcher's cabin deep in the countryside for beers and burgers. Fletcher was good with a spatula, and he flipped the hamburgers on the barbecue with a certain care, concern, and affection that could only come with military training. It has been my experience that military personnel are almost always excellent barbecue chefs.

We eat the burgers in silence, where after Fletcher places a dossier labelled "secret" on the clean kitchen table.

FLETCHER That corn? That corn could have fed hundreds of people, and it was destroyed.

LUMIERE Destroyed?

FLETCHER Destroyed. There were exactly sixteen twisters in that section of corn within a month. The meteorological chances of that happening are so astronomically small as to be nearly impossible.

LUMIERE Wow....

FLETCHER Wow is right. They're trying to kill us.

LUMIERE Who?

FLETCHER The government, that's who!

LUMIERE Fletcher carefully opens the dossier, and shows me a number of documents. He believed these documents were evidence. Evidence that the CIA and the Pentagon had been secretly manipulating weather systems. With the silent support of the government.

FLETCHER They're starving their own people.

LUMIERE Why?

FLETCHER To test this weapon they know they can't test anywhere else. No different than nuclear testing or chemical warfare. Weather Warfare. It's the next thing.

LUMIERE I don't know, Fletcher, don't you think the weather's pretty much a random thing?

FLETCHER That's what I used to think… that's just the way I used to think….

• • •

LUMIERE Once upon a time, there was a teenager. This teenager belonged to a family who lived in a small- to medium-sized home, in a small- to medium-sized city, in a western province, in a place known as Canada.

The city the teen grew up in was a normal kind of city, and the home the teen grew up in was a normal kind of home, with all the normal, small- to medium-sized home-like features.

With two exceptions:

Number one: The teen had a brother. A twin. And until he was sixteen, the teen shared a room with this twin brother.

Exception number two: The home of the teen was also the business office of the teen's parents, who were morticians. Or funeral directors, as they liked to call themselves. It was their job to look after people in times of bereavement and grief, and so the teen's home was an important and unusual home.

There was a kind of tunnel.

It connected the house to the funeral home. So that in order to get to the office of the funeral home, one would have to go through the tunnel. And in this tunnel was the "prep" room, or embalming room.

The teen brothers loved and feared the prep room.

Once, the boys were sent to get the Thanksgiving turkey from the deep freeze, which because of the necessity for constant cool conditions, was naturally located in the prep room. Quickly and quietly, the brothers carried the frozen bird across the clean porcelain tiles gleaming under bright fluorescent lights.

Oft times, the faint and muffled cries of grieving customers travelled from the funeral office down the tunnel toward them. Now and then, the brothers peaked through the door to catch a glimpse of their parents "dressing" the body, preparing it for burial. Like juice through a straw, the brothers watched blood drain from the cadavers, and replaced with fluids to better preserve and present them.

Contrary to popular belief, the household of the mortician parents and their twin sons was one full of mirth and levity. The parents loved their sons, the sons loved each other, and often the family would play jokes on each other.

Like the time dinner guests were over, and all had retired to the living room for coffee, when suddenly, an eyeball rolled out into the middle of the floor. The guests were transfixed with horror, the parents with embarrassment. One teen bent down and touched it gingerly. Then, he popped it in his mouth.

A gasp from all.

"It's glass!" the teen said, then popped it from his mouth and threw it to his twin brother, where after they proceeded to play catch with the glass eyeball. When it was realized that this was nothing more than a teenage prank, and that no morbidity was meant, the family and guests all had a good laugh at death.

When the teen was sixteen, he took an abrupt interest in his parents' work and learned the family trade—its fascinating history and business practices. He learned to polish coffins, drive the hearse, coordinate grave-site activities, and assist in prep work.

Pause.

Years later… when the parents died unexpectedly, the teen, now a man, insisted on performing the prep himself. The parents had died a violent death and the bodies were not cooperative, making the reconstruction, dressing, and embalming procedure a distressing affair.

Slowly, and with great care, the son washes and cleans his mother, manicures her nails, applies her makeup, perfumes her skin, and dresses her in the pantsuit she loved to wear.

He creates a smooth lather, and dipping the razor in the water, brings the blade to his father's chin. Tears race down the son's skin to his father's, as he scrapes away the final stubble of life.

The son works late into the night.

He speaks to them.

Chastising them.

Reassuring them.

Telling them things he never before dared to voice.

"I love you… I love you so…."

He washes his hands and cleans the instruments. Calls are made: priest, florist, cemetery, stone cutters. Obituaries are written and caskets chosen. Then he lays his parents to rest on a bed of the finest oak.

Finally, dirt is thrown on the caskets, and the oak once more takes root in the earth below.

> *LUMIERE leans on a chair. The ASSISTANTS enter with razor, water, mirror, etc.*

You don't mind if I rest for a moment, I hope. You should never see a caterer sitting. Ever. It is very bad manners and can be very disturbing to the customers. But, please, don't be alarmed.

LUMIERE sits. The ASSISTANTS give him a shave.
LUMIERE meditates. Another ASSISTANT enters.

ASST.   Sir?

> *Pause.*

Sir?

> *Pause.*

Sir?

LUMIERE   WHAT?!

> *Pause.*

WHAT?!

> *Pause.*

I'M BUSY! CAN YOU NOT SEE THAT I AM BUSY?!

ASST.   *(glances at watch)* Sir....

LUMIERE   How long?

ASST.   Ten minutes or so, sir.

LUMIERE   Right.

> *Pause. LUMIERE gazes at himself in the mirror. He*
> *turns to the ASSISTANTS.*

Thank you.

> *The ASSISTANTS leave.*

The main course will be served shortly.

• • •

LUMIERE   A long, cold, dark day. A dusty rural road. A big sky.
A big hunger. The van barrels across the northern
prairie toward Flin Flon. Dust and gravel fly. I pull
into the five-star motel—five stars because it's the
only one in town.

And I say to myself, I say: "Why? Why in Christ's
name did I become a Schwann Meat salesman?"

"Because I love it," I tell myself, and I have yet another drink. The pinball machine whines. The darts are thrown a little too hard. The solids and stripes break against my brain like a hammer against the minerals and rocks that support this scuzzy town. This town....

WAITRESS How's everything?

LUMIERE The same question, in every town, at every lunch, at every dinner.

Never eat in the Chinese restaurants. Don't assume you'll get brown bread. Make sure it's not really Tang. Salads cost ten dollars—they've got to fly in the lettuce, we're so far north. Always order the clubhouse, it's the hardest thing to get wrong. The waitress comes by.

WAITRESS How's everything?

LUMIERE "It's fine," I used to say, when I first started this job. "It's fine," I say, as I swallow another clod of rancid veal cutlet, another order of synthetic mashed potatoes, another glass of instant milk.

"It's fine."

Sixteen months after my first meeting with Fletcher; sixteen months after giving the Young Conservative thing another try; after sixteen months trying to sell Schwann Frozen Veal Cordon Bleu, Schwann Frozen Pork Chops, and Schwann Frozen Chicken Breasts to rural housewives with no dispensable income; after sixteen months, I have moved from one to thirty-five cigarettes a day, from one drink after work to.... After sixteen months, the waitress asks me:

WAITRESS How's everything?

LUMIERE And for some reason, I say, I say: "Not very good, really. Not very good at all. These potatoes are awful." The shock on her face—unforgettable. I have turned her world upside down.

And I think: Ah hah! If only I could get a good meal;
if only I could eat and not consume; if only I could
serve and not just sell....

I could change my world.

Pause.

That night I am asleep.

"Hello?"

VOICE Lumiere?

LUMIERE Yes....

VOICE I have a message for you.

LUMIERE Yes?

VOICE It's your parents.

LUMIERE Yes?

VOICE There's been an accident.

LUMIERE Oh?

VOICE They're dead. Come back as quick as you can.

LUMIERE And I cry such tears of joy, I wail such lamentable
happiness, such overwhelmingly awful feelings of
felicity fill my soul that I go straight out to the local
Chinese restaurant, order the greasiest seafood dinner
on the menu, shovel down the fetid shrimp, pay, leaving a good tip, walk out the door, and throw-up my
entire life. I was saved. Death had saved me.

It was then I decided to go into catering.

*The ASSISTANTS burst in with trays of food and place
them near LUMIERE.*

• • •

*LUMIERE begins to prepare some of the intermission
entrees. His creations are simple, yet awe inspiring. He
prepares them with incredible ease in a cool detached
state. It is practiced, precise, and is not ostentatious in
any way.*

LUMIERE   Food has a way of sounding its purpose, its function, its taste or effect. "Steak" for example. Or: "Fish."

> *He continues working, relishing each word.*

Soup.
Oats.
Wiener.
Bread.
Squid.
Chicken.
Paprika.

> *Pause.*

Parsley.

> *He begins cutting parsley.*

Here's a story:

The year was 399 B.C., and the Greeks had just lost the Peloponnesian War. Needless to say, they were in a mean mood, looking for a scapegoat. Enter Socrates: old, ugly, cynical, and—most important of all—a philosopher, the greatest truth-teller of his time.

GREEKS   That damn Socrates, he's a liar! He doesn't believe in anything! Make him pay a fine!

LUMIERE   But good old Socrates, he refused to pay the fine. So the government took the next logical step: it decided to execute him. Sometimes telling the truth can get you killed.

The Athenian method of execution was a kind of suicide by lethal injection. A cup of hemlock. Pale and oily, liquid hemlock blocks the sensory and motor neurons, causing convulsions, respiratory failure and, ultimately, Death.

Slowly, Socrates drank the hemlock. Waiting... waiting for it to take effect. Some guests showed up to witness the public passing of their companion and mentor. Socrates, ever practical, asked them to kindly document his demise for posterity. He started to walk in circles, hoping to quicken the poison's path through his system. After a time, Socrates weakened and lay down on a cot kindly provided by the Athenian penal system. The poison spread—to his feet, his hands, his lips. He had a series of long, beautiful convulsions and... died.

Killing rats on the Alberta/Saskatchewan border trained me in a plethora of poisons:

He relishes them.

Caustic potash.
Chloroform.
Fungi.
Curare.
Paraquat....

Such beautiful names. But the greatest and oldest, and my most favourite of them all, is hemlock. Because....

Pause.

Well, because it can be so easily mistaken for parsley.

He takes a bite of the parsley.

An ignition of lightning.

• • •

LUMIERE The boy dreams. Inside a fish bowl too small. Watching, as silent, formless shadows float by the faded glass.

Entering a tunnel.
Floating through.
Trapped inside.
Screaming.
Screaming for...
Screaming for his brother.
"I love you. I love you so."

• • •

LUMIERE Enjoy your meal. But don't eat too fast. Digest the
evening slowly. We wouldn't want you to get sick,
now would we?

> *LUMIERE exits. The ASSISTANTS cater the meal,
> during which the intermission takes place.*

ACT TWO

After the intermission, the guests are invited back to their seats by the ASSISTANTS. LUMIERE walks in and mingles with guests. Eventually, he takes a bite of food. He spits it out violently.

LUMIERE WHAT IS THIS??

The ASSISTANTS look to LUMIERE.

WHAT IS THIS??

He slowly pulls something from his mouth. The ASSISTANTS are horrified.

Go look!

The ASSISTANTS look at each other.

GO!!

The ASSISTANTS leave.

Pause.

My apologies. I am so terribly sorry. What has just occurred is a catering nightmare. Finding hair in one's meal is absolutely revolting. A meal is a ritual. It is sacred, and I don't like the idea that anything might disturb its purity.

Then again, the unfortunate truth is that before it hits your plate, food is treated as anything but sacred.

(to a guest) That carrot you're eating.

If you consider the time it died being the time it was picked, you are eating something that died three weeks ago. It was cleaned, cut, and sent to your grocery store via a plane, or most likely a truck. We paid it homage when we sautéed it in butter, we gave it a good old-fashioned wake when we served it, we placed it on a fine coffin—a plate—and when you shovelled it into your mouth, you buried it six feet under. And like worms nibbling the crust of a corpse, the enzymes in your stomach gnaw at the remains of the carrot, feasting on the chemicals that keep your body alive, while separating the leftovers into a rich, compact fertilizer called... poo.

But we don't like to think of it that way, do we? And so we dice the carrot instead of cutting it, we pour on the vinaigrette to disguise the vegetables; we create sauces to enhance the meat; we wrap it, we can it, we pickle it, freeze it, fry it, broil it, bake it, mash it, poach it, grind it, grill it, blend it, toast it, mince it. Make it beautiful, make it live again, like a mortician, using just the right amount of make-up, resurrects the corpse, makes the dead seem appetizing, seem good to... to....

• • •

LUMIERE   Once upon a time, there was a young boy who lived in a small- to medium-sized home, in a small- to medium-sized city, in a western province, in a place known as Canada. Every evening, the boy's mother carefully created dinner to the rhythm of the boy's father turning the pages of his newspaper.

One evening, the family sat down and dug into large helpings of scalloped potatoes, fresh carrots from the garden, and roast chicken. As the young boy picked up a drumstick, he could not believe his incredible luck. While the parents used cutlery to wrestle with their thighs and breasts, the young son said: "Look Mom, look Dad, I don't need a knife and fork. I've got meat with a handle."

A pause descended on the table. The young son thought this natural, that meat came with or without handles. The boy's twin laughed, and even the mother could not suppress a smile. The father, however, stood up, and without finishing dinner said: "Come with me."

Father and son travelled in silence. The son feared that he had said something terribly wrong, wondering: "Where is Dad taking me?"

Father and son entered a shop.

"Wait here."

The boy did as he was told, taking in the dimly lit surroundings, and plugging his nose against the overwhelming smell of... something. He wasn't quite sure what it was, but the smell was strong, and made his tummy turn.

The father returned with a man.

"Come 'ere," said the man. The boy, holding his father's hand, followed the man down a long tunnel and through a door. The boy could not believe his eyes: in front of him lay a room filled with animals. Sides of beef, legs of lamb, and fresh fowl. All of them dead.

"Come 'ere."

The father nudged his son, who stepped forward, the knot in his stomach growing. The man took a chicken, freshly plucked, and put it onto a cutting board.

"This is an animal. This is meat. It was once alive, and now it is dead."

With that, the man brought down the blade hard. The boy felt the knot in his stomach grow tighter. The man quickly and efficiently gutted the bird, letting the insides steam out.

The son watched the blood ooze, he saw the chicken's eye look dark and dead, he had visions of his own death, felt the blood drain from his face, and as the smell of innards reached the sensitive nerves of the young boy's nose, he leaned over, and threw up on the butcher.

And so a mother's meal was wasted.

But a valuable lesson was learned.

• • •

An ASSISTANT enters with a piece of paper and a pen.

ASST.   Sir?

>   *Pause. The ASSISTANT lingers.*

LUMIERE Yes?

ASST.   As you requested, sir.

LUMIERE Ah.

>   *LUMIERE reads. The ASSISTANT waits.*

Hmmmm.

>   *LUMIERE scratches out a word.*

Hmm.

>   *He writes on the paper. He hands it back to the ASSISTANT.*

Change this.

>   *The ASSISTANT stares.*

Change this.

>   *The ASSISTANT stares.*

Change it, or they won't understand.

>   *The ASSISTANT takes the paper, lingers.*

Thank you.

>   *The ASSISTANT exits. LUMIERE pours himself a large glass of wine. The ASSISTANTS clear plates.*

It is highly unusual for a caterer to drink with his guests. Usually I save such an indulgence for after the event, when the guests have happily strayed home, full, but wanting more. I pour myself a generous glass of Merlot, and sit down to evaluate the evening: What dish could people not get enough of. What dish didn't anyone touch. Did people enjoy themselves, or were they thoroughly bored, etc.

>   *He takes a sip of wine.*

I take the magnificent mounds of dirty dishes, the half-eaten platters of rotting fish, the glasses caked with calcifying red wine, the smeared cutlery, the creased linen—I take all this glorious waste to the back room. I sit amongst the mess, soaking in the rays of a successful event I have been responsible for, but haven't had time to witness. I sit, close my eyes, and nibble on the leftover sounds of the evening: business deals closed and love affairs started, toasts raised and cutlery dropped.

We spend a large part of our existence making things dirty: our clothes, our dishes, our love lives. We spend an even larger percentage of our life cleaning up: clothes, dishes, love lives. Then there is that small percentage, that unique twilight time, that special moment, when we don't clean or filthify, but... watch.

LUMIERE leads the ASSISTANTS in a chant.

Dirt
dirt
dirt.

Dirt
dirt
dirt.

Dirt.
dirt.
dirt.
dirt
watch.

Pause.

Dirt
dirt
dirt.

Dirt
dirt
dirt.

Dirt.
dirt
dirt.

clean.
dirt.

Pause.

Clean
dirt
clean.
Clean.
dirt
clean.

Clean.
dirt
clean
clean
clean.

Pause.

Clean
clean
clean.

Clean
clean
clean.

Clean.
clean
clean
clean
watch.

Pause.

Clean.
dirt
clean.

Dirt
clean
dirt.

Dirt
dirt

clean
clean
dirt.

> *Pause.*

Clean
clean
clean.

Dirt
dirt
dirt
watch.

> *Pause.*

Watch.

> *Pause.*

Watch.

> *Pause.*

LUMIERE Anyway.

> *Pause.*

We spend so much time making a mess of our lives.
Or trying in vain to clean it up. We rarely take the
time to just....

> *Lightning flares.*

• • •

LUMIERE The boy hears the wind whisper his name. He stands at
the window, and watches the lightning cast aquarium
shadows through rain-smeared curtains onto the floor
of his room.

Thunder. His twin brother mumbles, lost in dreams.
He turns on his back, his head pointed to one side.
The boy waits for lightning to show his twin's face.
He sees his brother's eyes move back and forth, sees
his lips speak soundless words, dreaming of birth, or

death, or both. The boy thinks, this is what I will look like when I die.

Another loud crack, and the brother jolts up in his bed:
Screaming.
Shh.
Screaming.
It's okay....
Screaming.
What?
What?

No answer, but heaving with breath the brother collapses in the boy's arms. The boy holds his twin brother tightly, rocking him into a sleep as deep as death.

   A wind moans.

• • •

FLETCHER You see this....

LUMIERE Says Fletcher.

FLETCHER This could be the start of a twister.

LUMIERE And he's right. We are standing in a field outside Robinson, Texas. Dust blows up from the south. If it's warm enough out on the gulf, the wind spills onto the land, turns into a tornado, and makes its way as far north as Oklahoma, killing trees, livestock, people, almost everything in its path. Eventually it loses steam and... kills itself.

   Pause.

Fletcher points northwest of Robinson.

FLETCHER You see that up there, you see that?

LUMIERE I look, and see spirals of smoke rising from the remnants of the Branch Davidian compound near Waco. The week before, eighty men, women, and children died in a fire Fletcher claims the government started. On purpose.

FLETCHER To curtail free speech....

LUMIERE Says Fletcher.

FLETCHER To show their power, to make sure they had control.

LUMIERE I watch the rising steam of the compound.

The Romans embalmed their loved ones in balsam, aromatic salt, honey, and wax. As friends and family mourned, they lit the body on a gigantic pyre. The soul rose upwards with the smoke and ash, until it reached the gods....

FLETCHER You hear about that tornado in Edmonton?

LUMIERE Says Fletcher.

FLETCHER You hear about that?

LUMIERE Sure. My parents, they were killed in that storm.

FLETCHER No, not Edmonton, Alberta. I mean that one in Kentucky.

LUMIERE There's an Edmonton, Kentucky?

FLETCHER That's right. Now. Was there ever a tornado in Edmonton, Alberta before?

LUMIERE Not that I know of.

FLETCHER Ever been one since?

LUMIERE No.

FLETCHER You see? You see? That's because it was a test. To see how things worked. There was never a twister in Edmonton, Kentucky before either. You think that's a coincidence?

LUMIERE But—

FLETCHER Kentucky, Alberta, it's all the same, Lumiere. It's the government, that's who's done it.

LUMIERE But, Fletcher—

FLETCHER I know these things, Lumiere. I know. They got your
brother, they killed your folks, and God knows,
they'll get you, too. I can see it.

• • •

LUMIERE Once upon a time there was a man and a woman who
fell in love. They married, had twin sons, and lived
happily in a small- to medium-sized city, in
a western province, in a place known as Canada.

The man and woman worked hard their entire lives,
to give their twin sons everything they needed. They
taught them about life, and how to lead it. They
taught them about love, and how to give it. They
taught them about death. And how to accept it.

The man and woman finished their life's work, and
decided to enjoy the rest of their adulthood in what
we call retirement.

They sold their small- to medium-sized home, and
they purchased two new homes. One home was in
Arizona, to escape the cold; the other home was
a simple, sparse, and modest home in a trailerpark on
the outskirts of a city called Edmonton. The man and
woman travelled from home to home, enjoying their
retirement, enjoying the fact their children were...
taken care of. After all, the man and woman loved
each other.

Pause.

One hot, muggy Friday afternoon in late July, the
man and woman returned from visiting one of their
sons. He'd been in an accident, this son, and put in
a care home. They had visited him and had returned
to their trailer home to make an early dinner.

A storm gathers.

There had been strong winds, rain, and even hail, on
this hot, muggy, Friday afternoon in late July. The
man and woman noticed the green hue of storm

clouds on the way home, and hoped it would not destroy their weekend.

The man and woman entered their trailer home. The man read the newspaper and the woman made dinner, after which the man did the dishes and the woman read the paper. This had been their ritual, their symbol of love and commitment, ever since they could remember.

It was not long after the man had cracked open the paper and the woman had started dinner, that they heard the winds grow stronger, smelled rain in the air, heard hail on their roof, and stepped outside to examine their circumstances.

This is what they saw: debris raining down, wind tossing vehicles to and fro, homes on fire....

No sooner had the man and woman raced back into their home, than the lights went out and they heard a sound like a freight train passing outside. The man and woman fell to their knees and crawled under the table. They crawled under the table, held each other tightly, rocked each other back and forth, praying to God and each other, praying:

"I love you. I love you so...."

And then it was over. And a call was made to notify the next of kin, which was me. They told me my parents were dead, there had been a tornado, an accident, they were dead, and "please come home as soon as you can," my parents were dead. They're dead.

• • •

LUMIERE Some time later, I phoned Mila Mulroney.

He takes out a small picture of MILA.

She had helped me before. She had told me "Serve others, and others will serve you," which I was trying to do.

I would call, to ask for relief funds, to ask about what insurance policies would or would not cover, about how I could pay for funeral costs, and so on. I would call Mila to say: "my mother and father have been killed. And I don't have money to bury them. And my brother is very sick. And I have no money to take care of him. And I don't want a handout, I don't. What I want is... what I want is...."

So I called. And left a message. And I called. And left a message. And I called again and left another message. And I called and left more messages. And I called, and called, and called, and left more and more and more messages. And I kept on calling, over and over and over, until the secretary said:

SEC.   I'm sorry. She's busy.

LUMIERE But she said that I—

SEC.   She says she doesn't know you.

LUMIERE But she told me to—

SEC.   She says she doesn't know you. And if she doesn't know you, she doesn't know you. Now please, don't keep calling or I'll notify the RCMP.

> *LUMIERE rips up the photo. An ASSISTANT enters.*

ASST.   Sir?

> *Pause.*

Sir?

> *Pause.*

LUMIERE Yes.

ASST.   Did you want us to....

LUMIERE Not yet. Soon.

> *The ASSISTANT leaves.*

• • •

FLETCHER I've got it all figured out.

LUMIERE Says Fletcher.

FLETCHER It's all coming together for me now.

LUMIERE Two years after I last saw Fletcher, we are driving down Interstate 33 through northern Oklahoma.

FLETCHER The government's after people—you know why?

LUMIERE Like you said, weather warfare.

FLETCHER No. The real reason they're after people, is to get people needing them. That's why. The government's using all these storms to kill the "real" food, so people will rely more on "fake" food: McDonalds, coffee whitener, you know. The less "real" food we have, the worse we eat, the more unhealthy we are, the less successful we are, the more our minds shrivel, the more we need the government, the more government jobs remain secure.

LUMIERE Right....

FLETCHER And you know why they're after you.

LUMIERE I... think so.

FLETCHER It's obvious. You're a caterer. You're interested in food, and not only that, you're interested in good food, and making that food look good. You see? It all makes sense.

LUMIERE We pass through Beaver County, crossing the North Canadian River. A half hour out of Oklahoma City, a state trooper pulls us over.

TROOPER Can I see some ID?

FLETCHER What seems to be the trouble, officer?

TROOPER There's been a bombing. In Oklahoma City.

LUMIERE A... bombing?

And I see a bead of panic masquerading as sweat run down Fletcher's forehead onto his cheek. He hands over his licence, along with both our passports. The trooper heads back to his car to check us out. Fletcher turns to me:

FLETCHER   Oh, Jesus... Jesus.

LUMIERE   What, what is it?

FLETCHER   A couple of guys were talking, we were talking was all, about bombings, about taking action. Shit, and now there's you.

LUMIERE   Me?

FLETCHER   If they find out about you, about who you are, they're going to implicate me in this.

LUMIERE   What?!

FLETCHER   They killed your folks, they got your brother, they're after you, and now you're in my car!

    Pause.

LUMIERE   Fletcher and I are in a county jail for questioning. We hear about what has happened at the Murrah Federal Building.

    At lunch, Fletcher is eating fish. He starts to choke on a stray bone.

    All I do is watch.

    Fletcher is speechless. He cannot call a guard, and we are sitting far from other cellmates. He motions for me to help him.

    All I do is watch.

    I watch as Fletcher gags for air, his face goes blue, his bowels void, and his body slumps to the floor. A guard runs over and performs first aid. An ambulance is called.

    Twenty-four hours later, I'm allowed to leave. When they hand over my belongings, they ask how I feel.

    "Fine. Why?"

GUARD   Your friend there... Fletcher?

LUMIERE He's not my friend, I just hitched a ride.

GUARD Whatever, that Fletcher, they took him to the hospital.

LUMIERE How… is he?

GUARD Dead.

LUMIERE Oh.

> *Pause.*

> I had seen many dead things in my life, but I had never actually witnessed something—someone—die. I knew the beauty of food. I knew the beauty of death. Now I knew the beauty of dying. All you have to do is watch.

> *LUMIERE sits.*

• • •

LUMIERE I walk into the care home in the early evening, and go to your room.

> I stand by your bed, and watch the sun's lavender rays pass through avocado curtains and cast aquarium shadows on the floor. A family of fish in a bowl too small, the figures jump out of the bowl and splash to the linoleum, where they squirm and panic until the sun's setting terminates their lengthy, prolonged demise.

> You lie on your back, your head pointed to one side. Crisp sheets, cool on your pale skin. A highway of feeding tubes. You haven't tasted a meal in years.

> I sit on the chair beside your bed, my hands curled in my lap. Kids at school used to call you a vegetable. I hated that.

> *(slowly)* Hi.

> It's me.

> Sorry I didn't come earlier.

> Mom and Dad are dead, you know.

I don't have a lot of money, you see. I don't know how I can take care of you.

I'm not sure who did this to you: God, or the government, or the car…. It doesn't matter. What matters is… what matters is….

A storm summons.

There was a storm, you see. It was night, and there was a storm. And I got in my car, and I drove, just like you. I drove up along Highway 3, just like you. And I turned onto the gravel road, just like you. I went down a ways, and I came to the exact spot where you had your accident. And I stopped, and I got out of the car, and I lay on the road, in the pouring rain, just like you did, and I closed my eyes. And I thought about you, about your blood. Draining into the wet wheat, draining into the ditch, into the creek, into the Red Deer River, into the Bow River basin, all of that blood, reaching Drumheller, where you've been in this stupid care-home for sixteen years.

Silence: no hail, no thunder, no rain. Only a voice.

VOICE   Lumiere….

LUMIERE Yes?

And it spoke to me, not with words, but with ideas. Thoughts, concerns, beliefs, all spread out in front of me like a luxurious banquet. And I understood. I understood what Fletcher needed, and I understood what Mom and Dad needed, and I understand what you need. Someone to watch, to witness, to honour, to… to remember.

He produces a vial.

It won't hurt, I promise you….

Pause.

The teen, now a man, sits on the edge of the bed and moves close to his twin brother.

The man slowly takes his brother's head in his hands.

Leaning over, he opens his brother's mouth, and pours in the vial of crushed hemlock.

LUMIERE drinks the vial.

"I love you. I love you so."

He kisses his brother gently on the mouth.

He waits and waits, until he feels his brother's body convulse. Once. Twice. Three times. At last, he feels his brother's lips begin to cool. Wipes tears from his eyes. Holds him in his arms. Holds him for a long time, rocking him back and forth. Twins again.

An ASSISTANT enters.

ASST. Sir?

LUMIERE What.

ASST. Sir, perhaps we should....

LUMIERE Now.

ASST. Sir?

LUMIERE Now!

The ASSISTANT runs off.

● ● ●

LUMIERE I wonder if you would be so kind as to join me in a little toast.

To Mila.
To my dear friend Fletcher.
To my parents.
To my brother.
And of course, to you—my esteemed guests.

The ASSISTANTS return. They create a death bed with the catering table, linens, left-over food, cutlery, and other catering items. Then they complete the "prep": they help LUMIERE remove his jacket and replace it

> *with a new one; apply a deathmask of make-up; mist him with perfume.*

As you recall, I asked you here for several reasons. Number one: to eat. And I do hope you've enjoyed your fare. Number two: to listen. To my testament, my… life. And you have been so very patient in that regard, and I thank you. And number three, to watch, to… witness my passing.

The ritual is almost complete. The body has been prepped, the meal has been served, the obituary written.

> *The ASSISTANTS disperse small bags of parsley. Accompanying the parsley is a scroll with LUMIERE's obituary.*

Now that I have served you, I ask that you serve me. And to help you in this task, I want you to take something home.

> *During the dispersal of the obituary, LUMIERE slowly circles the death bed. He feels faint. He lays down on the table.*

I love you. I love you so.

> *LUMIERE has a series of slow, beautiful convulsions, and is dead. The ASSISTANTS stand vigil.*

● ● ●

> *On the scrolls that accompany the parsley, is written the following:*

This evening, between the hours of eight and ten p.m., Lumiere, renowned caterer, political observer, student of philosophy, surrounded by acquaintances, after much deliberation, by his own hand, peacefully re-joined his loving family.

Guests were treated to an excellent meal catered by the deceased. Musical accompaniment provided a refined atmosphere, not only for the repast, but also for ~~re-living~~ witnessing the life and passing of the caterer. Dress was casual.

In lieu of flowers, please plant, consume, or share the parsley provided.

Lumiere is predeceased by his mother, his father, and his brother.

His body, soul, and history are survived by no one but you.

The end.

Vern Thiessen is one of Canada's most produced playwrights. His work has been seen across Canada, the United States, and Europe, including *Shakespeare's Will*, *Apple*, *Einstein's Gift*, *Blowfish*, *Vimy*, and *The Resurrection Of John Frum*. Vern is the recipient of numerous awards, including the Elizabeth Sterling Haynes Award for Outstanding New Play, The City of Edmonton Arts Achievement Award, The University of Alberta Alumni Award for Excellence, The Canadian Jewish Playwriting Competition, and the Governor General's Literary Award, Canada's highest honour for playwriting. He has also been nominated for several Alberta Literary Awards, and the prestigious Siminovitch Prize in Theatre. Vern received his BA from the University of Winnipeg and an MFA from the University of Alberta. He has served as Playwright in Residence at Workshop West Theatre (where he founded the Playwrights' Garage program), and the Citadel Theatre in Edmonton. He is a Past President of both the Playwrights Guild of Canada and the Writer's Guild of Alberta.